Introduction

If you asked your family or closest friends to name one of the great natural wonders of the world, they might choose you. But human beings, however miraculous they are, are not usually counted among the natural wonders. When we speak of natural wonders we mean certain features of or around planet Earth that are not manmade and that impress us with their awesome power, size or beauty.

Some of these natural wonders are the only one of their kind. Very many are rarities. Most of them, too, do not make up part of the daily experience of lots of people – often because they themselves form an environment that is unfit or unwelcoming for human habitation. Some of the most amazing landscapes, for example, are deserts or rock formations in deserts. Here the climate is generally too extreme for people to live comfortably and the land is often unusable either for crops or livestock.

On the whole, you will not find natural wonders on your doorstep: you will have to make the effort to go and see them. Their remoteness gives them an extra charm.

Another special aspect of natural wonders, however, is that you do not just see them. You can feel the bark of the giant sequoia trees of California or the stone surface of Wave Rock, Australia. Hear, from kilometres away, the roar of water tumbling over the Victoria Falls. Smell the sulphur fumes at the geothermal springs and pools of Rotorua. Taste the waters of the Dead Sea, a lake so salty you cannot swim in it.

The natural wonders in this book are divided into thirteen categories, each representing a type or environment. Some of these – for instance, Volcanoes, Freshwater and Air –

NATURAL
WONDERS

Ingrid Cranfield

AGON'S WORLD

DREN'S BOOKS

DRAGON'S WORLD

CHILDREN'S BOOKS

Dragon's World Ltd
Limpsfield
Surrey RH8 0DY
Great Britain

First published by Dragon's World Ltd, 1996

© Dragon's World Ltd, 1996

British Library
Cataloguing in Publication Data
The catalogue record for this book is available from the British Library.

ISBN 1 85028 317 6

Editor: Diana Briscoe
Picture researcher: Richard Philpott
Designer: Mel Raymond
Art Director: John Strange
Design Assistants: Karen Ferguson
                   Victoria Furbisher
DTP Manager: Michael Burgess
Editorial Director: Pippa Rubinstein

Typeset by Dragon's World Ltd
in Stempel Garamond and Gill.

Printed in Italy

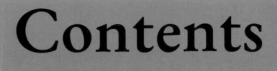

Contents

reflect the origins of the features. Others – such as Caves, Trees and Rocks – describe what the features look like. Of course, a picture speaks a thousand words, but some things cannot be shown in pictures. In the text we try to tell you something both about what you can and cannot see in the illustrations and to explain how each natural wonder came to be in its present form.

This book introduces you to one hundred of the most outstanding features of our Earth. Perhaps it will encourage you to visit at least one or two of them. More important, it may inspire you to work towards the conservation of this marvellous planet, itself the ultimate natural wonder.

Ingrid Cranfield

Opposite
Top left: The Ross Ice Shelf, Antarctica.
Top right: Giant Sequoias, California, USA.
Bottom: Western Erg of the Sahara, Africa.

Above: the Eisriesenwelt caves in Austria.
Below: Mont Fuji, Japan.

7

Auroras

Auroras are dazzling bands, arcs, rays or curtains of light that move across the sky in polar regions. In the north, they are called the aurora borealis or northern lights, and in the south, the aurora australis or southern lights.

No one knows exactly why they happen, but it is thought that they are the result of tiny particles of energy from the sun that become trapped in the earth's magnetic field. Every eleven years or so, the sun becomes very active, sending a large amount of energy particles out into space. It is then that auroras are at their most spectacular.

City lights and tall buildings on the horizon may get in the way of the display, so the best views of auroras are from country areas. In the town of Churchill in Canada, auroras are seen on about 300 nights of the year, whereas in the American state of Florida the average is about four times a year.

Most auroras appear between 90 and 130 km above the earth, but some are much higher. In 1959, an aurora borealis was measured at a height of 160 km and a width of over 4,800 km.

Auroras have been known for at least 2,000 years and have been the subject of many myths. In the early Middle Ages, the Vikings of Scandinavia believed that the auroras were warrior horsemen galloping across the sky. In the Arctic, the Inuit people thought they were created by spirits to light the way for people who had recently died.

▼ The aurora borealis, or 'northern lights', is seen here in the form of multi-coloured rays over Fairbanks, Alaska.

A fine display of aurora borealis in England in 1938 was mistaken by many people for a great fire like the one that destroyed much of London in 1666. During the Second World War, another display over the US capital of Washington, DC, in 1941, caused panic as it was thought to be the beginning of an attack by German bombers.

Barringer Meteor Crater

Some natural wonders are famous for their beauty. The Barringer Meteor Crater in Arizona, USA, is not one of them. It is an ugly scar on the desert caused by a meteorite hitting the Earth between 20,000 and 50,000 years ago. The crater is 1,264 m across, 174 m deep and is the largest impact crater in the world. There are others in Mexico, Antarctica, Australia and Siberia.

For some time after it was noticed in 1871, Europeans thought it was the collapsed top of a volcano. However, in 1902 Dr Daniel Barringer proved that the rocks around the hole were not volcanic and showed signs of having been crushed by some enormous body crashing into them with terrific force and at a speed of about 69,000 kph. The explosion would have been about forty times as large as the atomic bomb that destroyed the city of Hiroshima in Japan in August 1945.

A meteorite is simply a rock that has crashed into the Earth from space. The bigger the meteorite, the greater its impact. At first no-one could understand why the meteorite itself could not be seen at the Barringer Meteor Crater. Some people thought that it was buried under the ground. Then scientists realised that this 70,000-tonne rock, at least 25–30 m across, had smashed itself to pieces when it landed.

▼ A meteorite weighing about 70,000 tonnes smashed into the earth, creating the Barringer Meteor Crater and destroying itself in the process.

Scientists use the Barringer Meteor Crater for research and American astronauts have trained there because it is so similar to craters on the moon. Some visitors are also allowed. The crater floor can be reached by a steep trail, which takes an hour to walk down.

Ngorongoro Crater

Ngorongoro is a volcano in northern Tanzania that has been extinct for at least 250,000 years, and perhaps for as long as 2.5 million years. When it was still active, eruptions blasted away the peak of the volcano leaving a complete bowl-shaped crater that is the biggest in the world. The crater is 20 km across. The crater walls rise steeply 600 m from the valley floor.

Ngorongoro National Park, which sits in the crater, is one of Africa's most important wildlife sanctuaries. Between 25,000–30,000 animals live on the crater floor. In addition to zebras, gazelles, elands, leopards, jackals and wildebeest, there are huge numbers of black rhino.

There are many springs and a large, blue saltwater lake that never dry up completely, even at the hottest times.

▼ Aerial view of the Ngorongoro Crater, Tanzania, showing how the crater wall makes a natural enclosure for the game reserve.

The native people, the Masai, move about with their herds of cattle to find water and food. They measure their wealth in cattle and only rarely hunt for food or kill wild animals for their skins. The Masai are dignified and graceful. They redden their hair and wear rust-coloured robes knotted at the shoulder.

Mount Vesuvius

Mount Vesuvius rises 1,277 m above the Bay of Naples in Italy and is the only active volcano on the mainland of Europe. Its crater is 1,400 m around the rim, 216 m deep and more than 3 km across. It used to be known as Monte Summa or Somma, and part of the rim of that ancient mountain makes a half-circle around the present crater.

Vesuvius has erupted from time to time over 12,000 years. There are always wisps of smoke curling out of the crater and pockets of earth on its slopes that are hot enough to set a piece of paper alight. Its foothills are covered in orchards and vineyards, but the upper slopes are lonely and threatening. There have been six major eruptions in this century.

▲ A minor eruption from the lava-covered cone of Mount Vesuvius gives a warning of further, more violent eruptions to follow.

▼ Stormy weather over Mount Vesuvius, here seen behind Pompeii, the city it destroyed with its eruption in AD 79.

The most famous eruption was in AD 79, when the towns of Herculaneum and Pompeii were destroyed. The volcano belched out an enormous cloud of black smoke. Hot ash and stone rained down and poisonous gas spewed into the air. Only a quarter of the people of Pompeii escaped. The rest were buried in ash, choked by fumes or crushed by buildings.

Surtsey

Iceland is the world's largest landmass that was created entirely by volcanic action. It is surrounded by small islands also created by volcanic activity.

In November 1963, a fishing vessel was sailing to the south-west of Iceland when the crew saw a tall column of smoke rising from the water. They thought it was another ship on fire, but it was the birth of Surtsey. Later in the day, dark columns of ash and blocks of lava were churned up from the sea and a jet of steam rose 3,600 m into the air.

Within a few days, an island about 40 m high and 550 m long had appeared above the water. By late January 1964, Surtsey was 150 m high and 2.5 sq. km in area. Eruptions stopped in 1967.

▲ In 1970, fulmar gulls came to nest there. The first flowering plant, a mayweed, took root in 1972; grasses, wild flowers and sedges now grow there.

Surtsey means 'island of Surtur' in Icelandic. Surtur was the giant god who guarded the land of fire (Muspell) in Norse myths. It was believed that he would ride across the nine worlds, setting them all on fire, just after Ragnarok, the final battle between the fire and ice giants and the old gods of Asgard.

▼ Many volcanic eruptions created the island of Surtsey. This is a 'cock's tail' eruption, about 400 m high, photographed in February 1964.

Auvergne

Climb up to the top of the Puy de
Dôme in the Auvergne, 1,465 m above
sea-level, and you will see fifty more
peaks like the one you are standing on.
The Puy de Dôme is one of the best
known of the volcanic cones that can be
found in this part of the Massif Central
mountains of France.

Altogether there are hundreds of these
peaks (called *puys* in French). Some are
weathered into softly rounded hills,
others are as sharp as needles. Some have
craters with lakes, while others are
smooth-topped. The many hot springs
in the area show that pockets of magma
(molten rock) lie close to the surface.
The Puy de Sancy (1,885 m) is the
highest peak. It stands in the million-
year-old range called the Monts Dore.

▶ Puy de Dôme, the best-known of the volcanic
cones in the Auvergne.

▼ View from Puy Mary over the Parc Naturel
Régional des Volcans in the Auvergne.

In ancient times, the stronghold of the Arverni
tribe (from which the name Auvergne comes)
was near the present-day city of Clermont-
Ferrand. Their leader, Vercingetorix, united the
Gallic tribes against the Roman general, Julius
Caesar, in 53 BC. Although he won one battle,
he then fought the Romans in Burgundy, where
he lost and was taken prisoner.

Krakatau

More than a million years ago, a cone-shaped volcano formed in the sea to the west of Java in Indonesia. Over the years, eruptions destroyed the top of the mountain. New cones rose above the sea and made an island called Krakatau, 9 km long and 813 m high.

On 26 August 1883, a deafening explosion was heard and an enormous cloud of black ash filled the air. The next day the greatest explosion ever known ripped the island apart. Two-thirds of Krakatau simply disappeared. The noise was heard in Australia 3,200 km away.

More than 19 cu. km of rock were shattered into dust and thrown into the air. An area 280 km wide stayed in total darkness for two-and-a-half days. Tidal waves smashed villages on the coasts of Java and Sumatra – 36,000 people died.

▲ An engraving of the remains of Krakatau, copied from a photograph that was taken shortly after the volcano had erupted in 1883.

▼ In 1925 a small volcano cone appeared above the water. Further eruptions pushed this upwards, and it has now become a small island, 188 m high. It is called Anak Krakatau (Child of Krakatau).

The effects of the eruption were felt right around the world. Everywhere the temperatures fell because the dust blocked the rays of the sun. Magnificent red sunsets were seen as far away as London and the west coast of the USA. The sun and the moon often looked green or blue for a year afterwards.

Mount Fuji

Mount Fuji (Fujiyama in Japanese) is not only a natural wonder, but also a sacred place, honoured by Buddhists, who think it is the gateway to another world. The crater is known as Naiin (the Shrine). It is important, too, in Shinto, the ancient Japanese religion. Its followers believe that gods or spirits (*kami*) reside within rocks, trees and other natural forms.

Mount Fuji is also exceptionally beautiful, with its usually snow-capped, cone-shaped peak, its elegantly sloping sides and completely circular base, about 126 km round. Rising sharply from near sea-level, it can be seen up to 80 km away on a clear day. Mount Fuji is a young volcano that grew some 600,000 years ago. Eighteen eruptions have been known: the last was in 1707, when ash spread as far as Tokyo, 100 km away.

▲ Mt. Fuji at sunset.

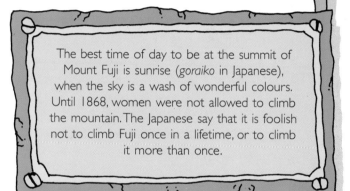

The best time of day to be at the summit of Mount Fuji is sunrise (*goraiko* in Japanese), when the sky is a wash of wonderful colours. Until 1868, women were not allowed to climb the mountain. The Japanese say that it is foolish not to climb Fuji once in a lifetime, or to climb it more than once.

▼ Mt Fuji seen in a different mood, with Lake Ashimo in the foreground. The red-painted gateway leads to a shrine.

Paricutín Volcano

On 20 February 1943 a farmer named Dionisio Pilido was tending his cornfield in the village of Paricutín, Mexico, when he saw a crack appear in the ground. There was the sound of thunder and the earth shuddered. Then the ground bulged up and smoke gushed out of the crack, followed by sparks that set some nearby trees alight.

An hour later, villagers gathered to see the red-hot rock ooze out of a hole at the end of the crack. By midnight lava bombs were bursting into the sky, and a cloud of ash was gushing out of the now much bigger hole. In the morning, there was a cone 10 m high. By midday, the cone was nearly 40 m high. By the following day, the unfortunate Dionisio had no farm left. What he and the other villagers had witnessed was the birth of a volcano.

▲ By the end of March five weeks after the eruption started, there was a 6,000-m column of ash and dust over the volcano.

▼ Lava from Paricutín Volcano buried this village, leaving only the church tower uncovered.

After a week, Paricutín stood 140 m high. There was a constant thundering roar and rock fragments were thrown 800 m into the air. The noise could be heard 320 km away. Villagers had to move away from the area, where some of the houses had been smothered. The volcano went on growing and spilling out lava for nine years until it was 410 m high.

Mauna Loa, Hawaii

Measured across its oval-shaped base under the sea, Mauna Loa, on the island of Hawaii, is 119 km from end to end in one direction and 85 km from end to end in the other. Its base is 4,975 m below the Pacific Ocean. Above sea-level, Mauna Loa towers to a further 4,170 m. Adding these measurements up, Mauna Loa is therefore the largest mountain in the world. Its area above ground covers more than 5,180 sq. km.

It is also one of the largest active volcanoes in the world. It has been built up to its present height with layer on layer of lava flows, and is active on average about every three years. An eruption in 1984 went on for twenty-two days. The lava from Mauna Loa is unusually hot and fluid, and flows very freely for distances as great as 32 km before it finally sets.

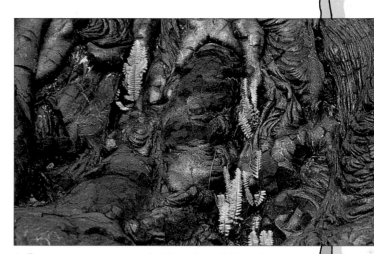

▲ Ferns grow among cooled lava from Mauna Loa.

Native Hawaiians believe that Pele, the fire goddess, came to live in Hawaii's volcanoes when she was driven away by her angry sister, the sea goddess. Fleeing from one volcano to another, she eventually found a safe home in the crater of Halemaumau on Kilauea island. The eruptions we see are said to be displays of her sudden tempers.

▼ A sea of lava stretches into the distance in Volcanoes Park, Hawaii.

Haleakala Crater

Haleakala Crater on the Hawaiian island of Maui is the product of many volcanic eruptions and of thousands of years of erosion by wind, rain and streams. All these forces have widened and flattened it to its present enormous size. It is 34 km around its rim, big enough to hold the whole island of Manhattan, USA, and 800 m deep.

Haleakala last erupted in 1790, so it is dormant – it could erupt again, but it has not done so for a long time. With its great depth and width, and a height above sea-level of 3,055 m, it is the largest dormant volcano in the world.

Inside the crater are hundreds of fallen rocks, cones of cinders up to 300 m high, layers of ash and volcanic 'bombs' or lava chunks ranging from the size of a hand grenade to as big as a car.

▶ Silversword grows to 1.5 m tall in the dry crater of Haleakala. Each plant flowers only every 10–15 years.

▼ Haleakala Crater seen from the air.

The nene or wild Hawaiian goose was once common in Maui, but was wiped out by animals such as rats and mongooses that had been introduced to the island by visitors. Pairs of nene were brought back to the crater in the 1960s and have since bred and thrived, although it is still a rare treat to see these birds.

Bora Bora

The American writer James A. Michener called Bora Bora in the Society Islands 'the most beautiful island in the world', and had it in mind as the setting for his novel, *South Pacific*, later made into a musical. For many people, it is a paradise on earth. The first inhabitants arrived from South-east Asia 2,000 years ago.

In the middle stands the remains of a volcano with twin peaks. Mount Otemanu, now 725 m high, used to rise 5,400 m above the sea-bed, before eruptions destroyed the top. This long-extinct (dead) volcano is now covered with thick, green forest.

Around this is a beautiful turquoise lagoon, which is separated from the sea by a sandbank. Beyond that, almost in a complete circle, is a barrier reef, dotted with small sandy islands called '*motus*'.

▲ Bora Bora sits like a jewel in the blue waters of the southern Pacific Ocean.

The English naturalist Charles Darwin was the first to realize that an atoll is a barrier reef that has grown up in a ring around an island. If the island sinks into the sea, the atoll is left behind. Bora Bora is sinking and one day only its atoll will remain. During World War II, the US government used Bora Bora as a refuelling base on the route to Australia and New Zealand.

▼ This picture shows the remarkably distinct line between the turquoise lagoon, the sandbank edging it and the surrounding ocean waters.

San Andreas Fault

The Earth's crust is not solid, but is made up of huge sheets of solid rock called 'tectonic plates'. Running through the American state of California is the San Andreas Fault, the fracture or break line between two tectonic plates. Here the North American Plate is moving northwards, while the Pacific Plate is moving southwards.

They grind sideways past each other at the rate of about 13 mm a year. Sometimes their passage is smooth and causes no disturbances. At other times, they catch or snag against each other, and as they break free they can cause a big earthquake.

The San Andreas Fault is 1,050 km long and stretches about 16 km below the surface of the ground. Much of it is hidden, but in places it leaves obvious scars in the land. Movements along the fault have sometimes been huge – on one occasion a stream on one side of the crack ended up 120 m away from the rest of the stream on the other side of the crack.

▲ The San Andreas Fault is at its most spectacular where it crosses the Carrizo Plain about 480 km south of San Francisco.

An earthquake in 1989 caused a 1.5-km stretch of elevated road to collapse on to the lower level of road. Cars and lorries were crushed and sixty-three people killed. The cost of damage to buildings, other structures and water and gas pipes was about US $7,000 million. About 20 million people live with the threat of earthquakes along the fault.

▼ There are frequent earthquakes along the San Andreas Fault. Here a freeway in Los Angeles has been badly damaged by the 1994 tremor.

Pamukkale

The Pamukkale hot springs flow out of the side of the mountain of Cal Dagi in western Anatolia, Turkey. They bubble out of the ground at 37°C and cascade down over a series of terraces, which are made of a white substance, calcium carbonate, carried in the water. There is a pool within each of the hundred or so terraces. The terraces are mostly brilliant white in colour, but some are yellowish or brown because of minerals in the water. Sadly, pollution from road traffic threatens to dull their colour.

Nearby are the ruins of Hierapolis, founded in 190 BC. It became a popular health spa for Roman sufferers from heart and skin disease and rheumatism.

▲ Swimmers enjoy the warm waters in the brilliant-white rock terraces at Pamukkale.

A hot spring in one cave gives off gases that smell bad and bring tears to the eyes. Strabo, the Ancient Greek geographer and historian, said they would kill a bull in an instant. Local people said the fumes were associated with evil spirits.

▼ Calcium carbonate carried in the water at Pamukkale gives the rock surface its amazing colour and sparkle.

Santorini

The island of Santorini, or Thera as it is sometimes known, lies in the southern Aegean Sea. Originally it was an almost round island built up by successive volcanic eruptions, but in 1680 BC the volcano staged a particularly spectacular blowout, completely destroying the island's centre and leaving a huge crater, or 'caldera', which filled with seawater.

Scientists have estimated that the blast destroyed a mountain around 1300 m high and shot about 100 cu. km of rock into the atmosphere. Traces of the fallout have been found in Egypt and all around the eastern Mediterranean. There is still an active crater on a small island called Nea Kameni in the caldera.

▶ Part of the caldera wall; the cruise ship gives some idea of scale. Note the black bands of lava.

▼ A reconstruction of Santorini before the great explosion and as it is today. The islands inside the ring have grown from volcanic activity since the blast.

Many historians think that the ancient Minoan civilization of Crete was seriously damaged, if not destroyed by the Santorini explosion. Crete lies only about 100 km south of Santorini. The disaster may also have been responsible for starting the legend of Atlantis – of a great civilization on an island that was destroyed by volcanic action.

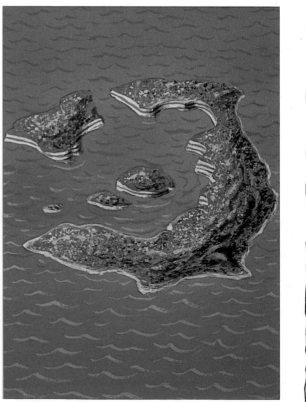

Strokkur

Strokkur is a geyser in the south-west of Iceland, about 80 km east of the capital, Reykjavik. Several times every hour, perhaps every 4–10 minutes, a dome of bluish-green, scalding water wells up over an opening in a pool about 3 m across. Then, with a roar, the bubble bursts and a column of boiling water hurtles 22 m or more into the air. The steam settles with a hiss and the waters calm down until the next eruption.

The original geyser, from which the word comes, is Stori Geysir (Great Gusher), in the same area as Strokkur. It used to be very active, but has quietened down and now gushes only occasionally. Geysers are found where magma (molten rock) lies near the surface. Water collects in underground pools where hot rocks heat the water.

▼ Iceland has 800 geothermal areas and hundreds of hot springs. It sits on the Mid-Atlantic Ridge, where two sections of the earth's crust are moving apart.

In Reykjavik, heating for factories and homes comes from natural hot water. People used to do their washing in hot springs and even bake bread in a hollow in the ground. At Hveragerdhi, nicknamed 'garden of hot springs', greenhouses heated by hot springs produce bananas, salad vegetables, grapes, orchids and roses.

If water can escape freely, it will come to the surface as a hot spring or mud pool. If it is trapped inside a natural pipe in the rocks, it heats up greatly and some of it is turned into steam under great pressure. When a head of steam builds up, a huge jet of water and steam shoots out of the ground. The process of heating the water and making steam goes on all the time, so after a while another jet of water and steam bursts out.

Old Faithful Geyser and Yellowstone National Park

Yellowstone is the oldest national park in the world (dating from 1872) and the largest in the USA. It mostly lies in the state of Wyoming. A volcanic plateau in the Rocky Mountains, it is full of mountains, lakes and forests. Other fascinating features are cliffs of black obsidian and thousands of geysers and hot springs.

'Geyser' comes from an Icelandic word *geysir*, meaning 'gusher' or 'rager'. Deep below the surface of the earth are very hot rocks. When these heat water to boiling point in a vent or tube, steam and water build up until they erupt out of the top. After the geyser's tube is emptied, it gradually fills up with water, and the whole process starts again. Old Faithful has been erupting regularly for at least 200 years. Every hour, about 45,500 litres blast up to a height of 30-45 m, in a five-minute display.

▶ Old Faithful, the best-known geyser in the world, has been erupting regularly for at least 200 years, always producing an impressive display.

▼ A wonderfully coloured hot spring in Yellowstone.

The most dangerous of the park's many animals is the grizzly bear. Now that so many visitors come to the area, they have lost their fear of humans and can cause accidents and even deaths when they come into contact with campers or walkers.

Rotorua

One of the most important areas of geothermal activity is Rotorua, in the North Island of New Zealand. Here there are hot springs, geysers, hissing steam vents and lakes of violently bubbling mud. Because there is a strong smell, it is nicknamed Sulphur City.

Just to the south at Whakarewarewa ('the place of rising steam' in Maori), is the country's largest geyser, Pohutu (or 'splashing'). It produces a boiling fountain up to 30 m high, sometimes minutes, sometimes months, apart. The display may last for up to 40 minutes.

To the east is Tikitere, where a Maori princess is said to have killed herself by throwing herself into the boiling pool. Hell's Gate at Tikitere is the only hot waterfall in the southern hemisphere and has a temperature of around 38°C.

▶ Whakarewarewa has this pool of bubbling mud.

▼ Champagne Pool is one of the marvels of the 'thermal wonderland' of the Rotorua region.

Up to 1886, visitors came to admire the pink and white terraces of silica. Then Mount Tarawera erupted with a noise that could be heard 160 km away and flames shooting 300 m into the air. Where the terraces had been, the explosions left a brilliant, emerald-green pool, steaming rocks and new terraces coloured green, brown, orange and black.

Lakes Natron and Magadi

Lake Natron in East Africa is the nesting-place of about 3 million lesser flamingos and about 50,000 greater flamingos. It is largely dry and made up of layers of sodium carbonate, or soda, lying on top of foul black mud.

There are several soda lakes in the area, but Lakes Natron and Magadi are the deepest and hottest and have the most soda. The temperature of the lake may get as hot as a bath, and the surface of the soda flat, the sludge around the edges of the lakes, where the flamingos breed, can be as hot as 65°C.

The crust of the lakes may be white, pink or pea-green, and the shallow water is often wine-red or coffee-coloured. The soda is washed in from the soil and from the nearby volcanoes. Spring water bubbling up maintains the supply.

▶ The soda crust surface of Lake Magadi, Kenya.

▼ A white heron, a pink flamingo and a pelican are feeding in the rich waters of Lake Natron, Tanzania.

The hot springs that run into the lakes are full of tiny fish called *Tilapia grahami*, which would die in cool water. In 1962, about 2,000 pairs of great white pelicans tried to breed in Lake Natron, but failed because the fish, on which the pelican relied for food, died. This was perhaps because the level of soda in the water from the hot springs became too high.

The Dead Sea

The Dead Sea is by far the lowest lake on earth, and the saltiest. The surface of the lake is 392 m below sea-level, and the bottom of the lake another 398 m below that. Ordinary seawater has about 3.5 per cent of salt in it. The Dead Sea has nearly ten times as much.

The Dead Sea formed in part of the Great Rift Valley, and is like a giant basin into which water flows. The temperature is so high that almost all the water (4–6.5 billion litres a day) flowing into it from the River Jordan dries up, leaving even more salt behind.

The water is deep blue and very calm, and so full of salt that you cannot sink or swim. Put one arm in and your other arm or a leg will bob up. If you want to dip yourself, you should lean back gradually until you are lying down flat.

▶ In this part of the Dead Sea, salt has built up into these strange shapes that look rather like snowmen.

▼ Salt is mined at the southern end of the Dead Sea.

According to old stories, the ruins of Sodom and Gomorrah lie at the bottom of the lake. The Bible tells that these two cities were burned down by God as punishment for their sinful people. Lot and his family were allowed to escape, but Lot's wife, disobeying God's instructions, glanced over her shoulder and was turned into a pillar of salt.

Salar de Uyuni

The Altiplano (or 'high plain') is a vast plateau in the Andes in Bolivia, never dropping below 3,000 m above sea-level. At its southern end are some salt lakes, left behind when ice melted and the water drained away at the end of the last Ice Age, about 10,000 years ago.

The biggest and most impressive lake is the Salar de Uyuni. Every winter it fills with rainwater to form a shallow lake. Every summer the water dries off leaving a crust of minerals, mainly salt, up to 6 m deep in the middle. You can drive across this surface, which gleams like a mirror, especially after rain.

Nothing grows there except for some cacti. Each lake is different in colour and texture from the others: red brick, green, turquoise or silvery-grey, depending on the minerals found in the salt.

▲ The Salar de Uyuni is the world's largest salt lake and lies about 3,700 m above sea-level in the Andes of southern Bolivia.

The surface of Laguna Colorado, another salt lake, is often completely covered by thousands of St James's flamingos, whose feathers are exactly the same shade of red as the lake. These rare birds feed on tiny plants called algae that live in the salty, near-freezing water of the lake.

▼ Here on the Salar de Uyuni, salt has formed into ridges, looking like honeycomb and stretching away into the far distance.

Lake Eyre

Lake Eyre, in central South Australia, is in fact two lakes. The larger is Lake Eyre North, 144 km long by 65 km wide. It is the largest lake in Australia. Lake Eyre South is 465 km long by about 19 km wide. The two are joined by the narrow Goyder Channel.

Lake Eyre varies in size enormously from 8,030 to 15,000 sq. km, but its average size makes it the nineteenth largest lake in the world. It is the lowest of the world's twenty-three largest lakes, lying about 11.8 m below sea-level.

The most extraordinary thing about Lake Eyre is that it very rarely has water in it. The rainfall in this part of Australia is less than 127 mm a year. Most of the time the lake is merely a dry bed with a crust of glistening salt, up to 20 cm deep. It is thought to fill up completely only twice every hundred years.

▲ Salt beds punctuate the waters of Lake Eyre North, the lowest of the world's largest lakes.

In 1964 the Englishman, Donald Campbell, set a world land speed record in his car *Bluebird* on the salt-flats of Lake Eyre. He reached a top speed of around 715 kph, about the cruising speed of a modern passenger plane. *Bluebird* was 9 m long and weighed 4,354 kg.

▼ Lake Eyre, here seen fairly full of water, something that happens only quite rarely.

Pitch Lake

When the English explorer, Sir Walter Raleigh, landed at Trinidad in the West Indies in 1595, he became the first European to hear about the 'Tierra de Brea' or 'Piche', where there was a large amount of pitch (bitumen or asphalt). We now know this as the Trinidad Pitch Lake, a weird but fascinating place and probably the largest deposit of pitch in the world.

The lake covers 44 hectares and is about 82 m deep. It was formed about 50 million years ago from the rotting remains of sea creatures. These made chemicals called hydrocarbons that filtered down through the rocks. Rock movements then forced them up to the surface of the earth, and they were then made solid enough to walk on by the heat of the sun.

The lake surface looks like a series of dark-grey folds, with hollows in between that collect pools of water when it rains. It is moving all the time, as the pitch oozes from the centre to the edges. There is the sound of occasional plops and bubbles as gas is forced out.

▶ The guide is drawing up a bubble of molten pitch.

▼ If you stand on the surface of the lake, your feet will sink in quite a long way, as they would in mud.

The Sumerians used pitch as a cement and the Babylonians used it as a waterproofing material for baths, stairways and pavements.
The Trinidad Pitch Lake has been quarried for over 100 years, but there are no scars to show for this, as the pitch just oozes back into any trench and fills it up.

Petrified Forest

Within the Painted Desert of Arizona, USA (see page 105), is the Petrified Forest – a widely scattered collection of logs and trees that have turned to stone. They were formed when silica from volcanic ash, dissolved in water, seeped into the wood, turning to crystals. Other minerals added the brilliant colours that are now seen in these stone logs.

Some of the logs look as if they had been chopped with an axe for firewood, but they were probably cracked by earth tremors. The Agate Bridge (agate is a semi-precious stone) is a single log over a 12-m ravine. Its span stands free, but both ends are buried in sandstone. Rock collectors used to do a lot of damage in the Petrified Forest, which is now protected by law. Now nobody may take away even a chip of stone.

▲ Logs and trees that have turned to stone (or petrified) are scattered over the valley floor among these horizontally striped mountains.

The Native Americans have a story to explain the existence of the Petrified Forest. A goddess was collecting wood to make a fire for cooking but the wood was damp and would not burn. She was so angry that she put an evil spell on the logs, turning them to stone so that they would never be of any use to anybody.

▼ An area of the Petrified Forest called Blue Mesa, where the petrified stones look as if they have been chopped with an axe.

Blue Holes of Andros

Andros is the largest of the islands of the Bahamas in the Caribbean. On its eastern side a long channel of deep water known as the Tongue of the Ocean curls past the shore. In places along this channel, there are shallows and coral reefs, and then sudden openings to great dark depths. These are the mysterious blue holes – entrances to some of the most amazing underwater caves and passages in the world.

Running water erodes (wears away) limestone rock relatively easily to form caves and tunnels. Bahamian limestone is the thickest known anywhere, stretching down 8 km beneath the sea. Coral reefs formed on the limestone, and as the limestone began to sink (about 1 cm every hundred years), the coral built up. Caves and passages formed – some are known to exist at depths of over 3,050 m and to be well over 2,300 m long.

The Bahamians call the blue holes boiling or blowing holes, because of the fierce tides that sweep in and out of the cave entrances. When the tide rises, the water in the openings to the caves starts to swirl round in a whirlpool, which will suck down anything. As the tide falls, the holes spew out mushroom-shaped domes of water. Exploring the caves can be very dangerous. The flow of water is so strong that divers can only enter at 'slack water', a calm period lasting only twenty minutes. Several divers have died in there by running out of oxygen.

Some local people believe that a monster called the Lusca lives in the blue holes. Half shark, half octopus, it is supposed to drag food with its long tentacles into its lair beneath the sea and spit out the unwanted remains. This is how they explain the violent movement of water in and out of the caves.

◄ This photo, taken from the *Apollo 9* spacecraft in 1969, clearly shows the deep blue Tongue of the Ocean curling down past the island of Andros. Andros and its surrounding waters are famous for their great caverns in the ocean floor – the blue holes.

The Maelstrom

In a channel in the Lofoten Islands off the north-west coast of Norway is a large powerful whirlpool called the Maelstrom. It first appeared on a map in 1595. Later it was made famous by the American author, Edgar Allan Poe.

People thought that whirlpools were caused by water running out through a hole in the sea-bed, and that they were so deep that no one could measure them. But the deepest part of the channel, where the Maelstrom spins, is 36 m deep, and there is no sea-bed hole.

The Moskenstraumen channel is about 8 km wide, with a bumpy bottom of rock and sand, which rises sharply from west to east. Tides sweep in from the west towards Norway and then fall back. As the tide comes in, the water is forced through the narrow channel. Bursting out on the coast side, it whirls around and squeezes its way back again.

The Maelstrom is caused by streams of water at the north, middle and south of the channel travelling at different speeds in different directions. Steep breaking seas and vicious currents make it impossible for a small boat to pass.

▲ The churned-up waters and whirlpools of another danger spot, Saltstraumen in Norway.

When it is at its most furious, the Maelstrom produces several different whirlpools at the same time. The noise of the winds that whip up the rough waves is frighteningly loud, half-way between a shriek and a roar.
'It is more appalling,' Poe wrote, 'than even a great waterfall such as Niagara.'

▼ An artist's fanciful impression of the Maelstrom, which lies near the Lofoten Islands, off the Norwegian coast. It was drawn in 1678.

Sargasso Sea

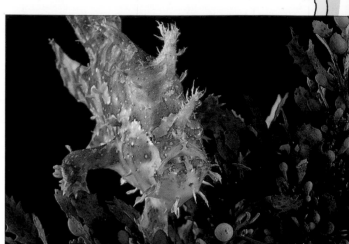

For over 2,000 years, stories have been told of ships being stuck in seaweed, and of sailors being dragged to their deaths in an area of the Atlantic Ocean between Bermuda and the Leeward Islands. Christopher Columbus, on his voyage to the Americas in 1492, was probably the first to sail into what we now call the Sargasso Sea.

The drifting rafts of plants are mostly made up of gulfweed, or sea holly (*Sargassum natans*). It is unusual because it does not live on or near the rocks of coasts. Instead it drifts in the ocean in large 'rafts' and spreads by breaking into pieces, which then go on growing independently.

The Sargasso Sea measures about 5.2 million sq. km, about twice the size of Argentina. To its north is the Gulf Stream current, which flows east, while to the south are currents that flow west. Their movement causes the Sargasso Sea to turn slowly clockwise.

▲ The gulfweed is home to this unfriendly-looking sargassum fish (*Histiro histiro*). Also known as the actor fish, its camouflage colouring allows it to hide among the weed and ambush other fish.

Eels hatch from eggs in the Sargasso Sea. The larvae then swim to Europe or the USA, where they grow in rivers. Eight or nine years later, they migrate back to the warm waters of the Sargasso Sea, breed there and die. Nobody knows exactly how they find their way back over thousands of miles.

▼ The Sargasso Sea is choked with rafts of gulfweed.

Sea-bed 'Smokers'

Until the late 1970s, scientists believed that all life on earth depended on sunlight to survive. Then a team exploring the oceans near the Galapagos Islands in the eastern Pacific Ocean found a wonderland of amazing creatures living in complete darkness 2,600 m below the surface.

These creatures live around jets of hot water, called 'smokers', that burst out of vents (holes) in the sea-bed. These vents are found where seawater seeps into rocks through cracks in the sea-bed. There it is heated to 350°C by magma (molten rock) under the Earth's crust. Heating the water forces it up to the sea-bed and out through the vents. The weight of the water pressing down at this great depth is enormous – 100 times greater than the pressure in a car tyre.

The boiling water that spews from the vents is extremely rich in minerals, such as iron, manganese, calcium, copper, zinc and sulphides. Different amounts of minerals make some of the smokers black, others white. Sometimes minerals are deposited around the vents, building chimneys which can be up to 55 m high.

▲ Gas and boiling water escape through the vents.

▼ This painting shows three active 'smokers' and some of the animal life that lives around them, including deep-sea crabs, white tube worms and clusters of molluscs (grey shells).

The giant, bright-red tube worms that cluster around the vents grow to 3 m long. They have no mouth, gut or anus and so cannot feed in the ordinary way. Instead, bacteria inside their bodies convert sulphides in the water, sucked in through tentacles, into food. Other creatures of the 'smokers' are giant clams, mussels and colourless, blind crabs.

Phang Nga Bay

Phang Nga Bay, in southern Thailand, is a place of marvellous beauty. The bay's brilliant greenish waters are dotted with limestone rocks, some rising hundreds of metres straight out of the water. Many look like the humps of a camel, while others resemble turnips planted upside-down.

The limestone is riddled with caves and tunnels. Some of the walls of these are covered with ancient paintings of men, animals and fish. Other caves and passages have long limestone columns called stalactites hanging from their ceilings.

At Koh Pannyi (Flag Island) is a little fishing village, built on stilts and with a tiny mosque (Muslim place of worship) clinging to the cliff face. A little further south, there is a large number of rock slabs made, 75 million years ago, from masses of sea shells all squashed together as if by a giant rolling-pin. This is called Shell Cemetery, because the slabs look like gravestones.

▶ Khoa Ping Kan was given its nickname of 'James Bond Island' after it was used as one of the settings for the Bond film *The Man with the Golden Gun*.

▼ Phang Nga Bay in the evening light.

Phang Nga Bay was one of the locations used in the James Bond film, *The Man with the Golden Gun*, made in 1974, and tourists in long, narrow boats now follow Bond's route to Khoa Ping Kan (Two Islands Leaning Back to Back), an island split down the middle by an earthquake long ago.

The Great Barrier Reef

The Great Barrier Reef, off the Queensland coast of Australia, is the largest, most varied and beautiful – and also one of the youngest (only 500,000 years old in places) – barrier reef in the world. It stretches more than 2,000 km from just north of Brisbane to the Gulf of Papua. It is made up of some 3,000 coral rafts and small islands, some only a few metres across, others as large as 50 sq. km. It spreads out into the Pacific Ocean for up to 330 km and altogether takes up a sea area of about 259,000 sq. km.

The Reef is most famous for its coral, although that makes up only about one-tenth of the reef's life. Coral is the skeletons of dead sea creatures called marine polyps. There are at least 350 different types of coral on the reef, of many different shapes, sizes and colours. Marine polyps are very fussy about their environment. The water must be warm (at least 22°C), turbulent (full of movement) so that it carries air bubbles, and clear because mud would block the coral's digestive system. They also need salt to survive.

In the 1960s and 1970s, the Great Barrier Reef was threatened by growth in the numbers of the crown-of-thorns starfish, which ate the coral polyps, so killing the Reef. Conservationists now have this problem under control, although the Reef will take time to recover. A marine park, covering 348,700 sq. km, established in 1979, protects the Reef from damage by visitors.

▼ There is hardly a more colourful or varied sight on Earth than the marine life in the waters of the Great Barrier Reef.

The Shipwreck Coast

Before the days of modern aids to navigation, seafarers used to fear the coast of Victoria, Australia more than any other stretch of water along the continent. The surf is rough and there are rocks, pillars and cliffs everywhere, both visible and hidden beneath the sea. The coast is about 320 km long. A 120-km stretch, nicknamed the 'Shipwreck Coast', has been the scene of more than eighty major shipping disasters.

The cliffs were once part of the sea-bed, formed of shells, mud and limestone. At that time, some 25 million years ago, the sea-bed was about 100 m higher than it is now. When the water dropped, they became the coastline. The stone stacks called the Twelve Apostles were once part of the mainland, but were separated by wave power.

▲ The Twelve Apostles were once part of the mainland until the waves eroded the land in between. Some have now crumbled away completely.

At Warrnambool along this coast is a viewing area for the 'whale nursery'. Southern right whales gather round the coast in winter to calve. The calves weigh 4–5 tonnes at birth and are extremely playful and entertaining to watch. These whales were given their name by early whalers, who thought of them simply as the 'right' whales to catch.

▼ The Pacific Ocean has carved stone stacks and eaten inlets into the southern coast of Victoria.

Reversing Rivers

The St John River rises in a pond in a wilderness area of north-western Maine in the USA and ends 39,673 km downstream in the Bay of Fundy in New Brunswick, Canada. Here there are enormous tides – the change in water level between low and high tide can be as much as 5 m.

At high tide, a wall of water is forced into the river's mouth and flows upstream, climbing about 5 m up a span of rapids called the Reversing Falls. When the tide turns, the river flows down normally to the sea again.

The Tônlé Sap, a river in Kampuchea, changes its direction at different times of the year. It flows between the Tônlé Sap Lake and the Mekong River, which is the longest river in South-east Asia and the seventh longest in all of Asia.

In midsummer, when the Mekong River is in flood, water flows up the Tônlé Sap to the lake, which then triples in size. In midwinter, when the floods subside, the Tônlé Sap reverses its flow, draining into the Mekong River.

▼ The Severn Bore, shown here at Stonebeach, Gloucestershire, is a wall of water formed when the incoming tide meets the outflow of the river. This phenomenon happens every day.

A 'bore' is a high, steep-fronted wave that rushes up a river from the sea when there is a very high tide. There is a bore called the Mascaret in France on the Lower Seine between the sea and the city of Rouen. Britain's longest river, the Severn, also has a tidal bore.

Victoria Falls

One of the world's greatest waterfalls, the Victoria Falls lie on the Zambezi River, which forms the border between Zambia and Zimbabwe. Upstream, the river flows slowly through a wide, shallow valley. You can be 40–65 km away from the waterfalls when you see a cloud of spray rising up to 300 m into the air. Long before you see the waterfalls themselves, you will hear the roar of the waters. The native people of the area call the waterfalls Mosi-oa-Tunya, which means 'the smoke that thunders'.

The Victoria Falls are formed by a deep rift in the rock that lies directly across the path of the Zambezi River. The rift was caused by movements of the Earth about 150 million years ago. At the widest point, the Falls are 1,690 m across. Facing the cliff where the river drops down is a second cliff, only 75 m away. Between them is a narrow gorge, where the water forms a huge whirlpool called the Boiling Pot. Then follow 72 km of gorges.

▶ The narrow gorge above the Boiling Pot.

▼ The trees in the background give an idea of the immense width and height of the Victoria Falls.

There are actually five sets of falls on the site: the Eastern Cataract, Rainbow Falls where the gorge is at its deepest, Devil's Cataract, the crescent-shaped Horseshoe Falls, and Main Falls which are 60–100 m high. In 1855 the missionary and explorer David Livingstone became the first European to reach the Victoria Falls, approaching them by canoe.

Caspian Sea

The Caspian Sea is the largest body of inland water in the world. With an area of 371,800 sq. km, it is bigger than Germany, nearly as big as Japan, and one-and-a-half times the size of all five Great Lakes of North America put together. About two-fifths of the total area is in Iran, where it is named Darya-ye-Khazar. The rest is in Russia, and there it is known as the Kaspiskoye More. Altogether this great lake (which is actually not a sea) is 1,225 km long.

The Caspian Sea lies in a huge basin and is up to 1,025 m deep, although in the flat bed at the northern end it is only about 5 m deep. About three-quarters of the Caspian Sea's water comes into it from the River Volga, which drains the uplands to the north. No rivers flow out of it and there are no tides.

The surface is about 28.5 m below sea-level. This is lower than it was in the early nineteenth century when it was 22 m below sea-level. In other words, the lake is gradually losing water. This is not because of the climate, but because of the work of human hands. The water in the streams that used to feed the lake has been diverted to be used for other purposes, such as irrigation.

Dams have also been built, with the result that less water flows into the lake.

In recent times, the Russian government thought of changing the course of some of the rivers of Siberia so that they would flow south into the Volga instead of north as they do now. This would fill the Volga, which in turn would fill the lake providing more water for the production of cotton.

About 12 million years ago, the Black Sea, the Caspian Sea and the Aral Sea (to the north-east of the Caspian) were all part of a much larger sea called the Tethys Sea, which was also linked up to the Mediterranean. This linkage happened again for a short time about 2 million years ago.

▼ An aerial view of the winter shoreline of the Caspian Sea, the world's largest body of inland water.

Off the main lake and almost cut off from it by long, low sand spits is a huge gulf called Kara-Bogaz-Gol. The water that rushes into it quickly evaporates. The gulf's water, nowhere more than 10 m deep, is 35 per cent salt, compared with 1.3 per cent in the main lake and 3.5 per cent in the world's oceans.

Lake Baikal

Lake Baikal, a crescent-shaped lake in Siberia, 640 km long and on average 50 km wide, is the seventh largest lake in the world. It is the world's deepest lake, and contains one-fifth of all the earth's freshwater – as much as all the Great Lakes of North America put together.

At its greatest depth, it is 1,640 m deep. If you stacked the world's four tallest buildings one on top of the other at this point on the lake-bed, the television mast on the roof of the fourth would still be 58 m below the surface of the water. Although the waters are also extremely clear, so that you can see 40 m below the surface, these four buildings would remain out of sight.

The lake was formed when a deep rift or crack in the Earth's crust filled with water. More than 300 rivers flow into the lake, but only one, the Angara, flows

▲ View of the Strait of Olkhon, on the west coast of Lake Baikal, the world's deepest lake.

out. In the winter the water stays frozen to a depth of over 1 m for four or five months. Deep inside the lake, however, the temperature stays the same, at about 3.5°C.

Lake Baikal has a great variety of plant and animal life, three-quarters of which is found nowhere else in the world. There are 255 species of shrimp here, including some that are so pale as to be nearly white. Two species of fish in Baikal are completely transparent.

▼ Lake Baikal contains about a fifth of the world's fresh water and is home to a unique range of wildlife.

The only freshwater seal in the world lives in Lake Baikal. In winter, it breathes by chewing holes in the ice. Because of the seals, which normally live in sea water, people used to think that Lake Baikal was joined to the Atlantic Ocean by an underground tunnel.
In fact, the seals probably travelled up the rivers during the last Ice Age.

Lake Hillier

▲ Lake Hillier on Middle Island is strikingly pink in colour, but nobody knows why.

Off Western Australia's south coast is a group of over a hundred islands called the Recherche Archipelago. In the corner of one of these, Middle Island, nestling amid a thick forest of eucalyptus and paperbark trees, is a glistening, pastel, icing-sugar-pink lake. It looks like a giant, white-edged footprint on a green, thick-pile carpet.

In 1950, scientists made a study of Lake Hillier, trying to understand how it gets its amazing colour. They expected to find that it contained algae (very simple plants) in its salty water. However, there are no algae in Lake Hillier and to this day no-one can account for the lake's strange colouring.

The lake is about 600 m across and fairly shallow. The deep blue water of the Indian Ocean is only a short distance away, separated by a narrow strip of woodland, white dunes and sand. The lake has been mined for salt in the past, but operations ceased many years ago.

Lake Hillier was first seen and mapped in 1802 by Matthew Flinders, a British seafarer and explorer, who called there on his voyage east to Sydney. Between the 1820s and the 1840s, Middle Island was settled by a few sealers and whalers.

▼ The water of Lake Hillier is extremely salty, which perhaps accounts for its glistening surface, if not for its colour.

Amazon River

The size of the Amazon River in South America is hard to imagine or describe. It is easily the largest river in the world. Of all the water that runs off the earth's surface, the Amazon collects about one-fifth. It rises 5,240 m above sea-level in the Peruvian Andes, over 6,400 km from the Atlantic Ocean. The Atlantic mouth is 320 km wide and so much water flows out that it drives back the salt seawater for over 160 km. In the mouth is an island about the size of Switzerland.

Over 15,000 rivers flow into the Amazon. Seventeen of them are longer than the River Rhine that flows through Europe. The Amazon is deep enough for large ships to sail up to Iquitos, Peru's 'Atlantic seaport', 3,680 km from the Atlantic.

▶ Aerial view of a tributary of the Rio Negro in the Amazon system during the high-water season.

▼ Queen Victoria water lilies on the Rio Negro; the leaves can support the weight of a small child.

The Amazon has had a number of names. The first Portuguese explorers called it the Marañon because one complained that 'it is a *marañon* [maze] that only God could figure out'. In 1542 an explorer claimed to have met a native tribe whose warriors were tall, white women, who reminded him of the Amazons of Ancient Greece. From this comes its present name.

Encontro das Aguas

The Amazon River has over 15,000 tributaries (rivers which flow into it) along its 6,400 km length. Almost 22,400 km of waterway are navigable by ships, and several million miles are passable by canoe. Many of these tributaries are different colours because of the different minerals and chemicals they contain. Those that come from the west generally run brown, those from the north black, and those from the south blue.

The Encontro das Aguas (or the 'wedding of the waters') happens at the town of Manaus in central Brazil. It is where the Rio Negro, which rises in Colombia and is black, flows into the brown Amazon. The Amazon River at this point is also known as the Solimoes.

This phenomenon of two different coloured rivers merging and mixing their colours does happen quite frequently elsewhere.
One of the most famous examples is in Austria just outside Vienna where the green Morava meets the blue Danube.

▼ The Encontro das Aguas at Manaus where the Rio Negro, which is black, flows into the brown Amazon. Both rivers are flowing so fast that the waters do not mix completely for several kilometres.

Angel Falls

In 1935, a US airman named Jimmy Angel was flying over the highlands of Venezuela searching for gold. As he flew over Devil Mountain, he spotted some waterfalls. Two years later, he returned for a closer look, but his plane crashed and got stuck in a swamp. He and his companions spent eleven days fighting through the jungle to reach the falls. Jimmy Angel did not find gold, but he did find the world's highest waterfall, which was named after him.

About eighteen times the height of Niagara Falls, the Angel Falls drop 979 m from the grassy, flat top of Devil Mountain. The water first cascades 807 m on to a rock ledge, and then down a further 172 m, ending in a great pool 152 m wide at the foot of the mountain.

The rainforest in this area is so thick that it is impossible to reach the bottom of the waterfalls on foot. In the wet season, when the rivers are deep with rainwater, it is possible to travel there by boat. For the rest of the year, the only way to see the waterfalls is from the air.

Devil Mountain, or Auyan Tepui as the native people of the area name it, is a mesa or tableland, formed perhaps as long as 65 million years ago by upward movements of the Earth's crust. The mountain top was worn away by the weather into cracks and pits. Rain collects in these and then gushes over the mountainsides.

▲ The Angel Falls, the waterfall with the highest continuous leap in the world, of 807 m.

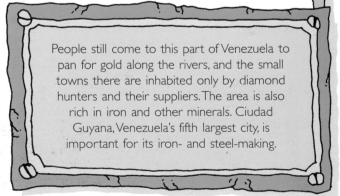

People still come to this part of Venezuela to pan for gold along the rivers, and the small towns there are inhabited only by diamond hunters and their suppliers. The area is also rich in iron and other minerals. Ciudad Guyana, Venezuela's fifth largest city, is important for its iron- and steel-making.

Lake Titicaca

According to the legends of the South American Incas, the greatest of the gods sent his children to find the best place to found the family line of the Incas. They chose the Isla del Sol (Island of the Sun) in Lake Titicaca, and a sacred rock marks the spot. A smaller island, the Isla de la Luna (Island of the Moon), is still thought of by locals as a holy place, and bears the ruins of a temple built for the worship of the Sun Maidens.

Lake Titicaca, covering an area of almost 8,800 sq. km, is nearly the size of Cyprus, and is the largest body of fresh water in South America. Sitting across the border between Bolivia and Peru, it is 195 km long and 100 km across at its widest point. It is also the highest navigable lake in the world. Its surface is 3,810 m above sea-level. Lake Titicaca is home for about 250 of the Uru people, who live on floating rafts built from a kind of papyrus reed called totora.

The Norwegian explorer and scientist, Thor Heyerdahl, noticed that the natives' boats, made of bundles of totora lashed together and rising to a high point at both ends, were very like boats used in ancient Egypt. In the 1970s, in *Ra II*, a boat made by Titicaca Indians, he sailed from North Africa to South America, proving that the Egyptians could have made the voyage.

▲ Aymara boatman paddling a reed boat on Lake Titicaca.

◀ Lake Titicaca, with the glorious mountains of the Cordillera Real in the background.

Iguaçu Falls

The Iguaçu (or Iguassu) Falls are the grandest waterfalls in the world, though not the biggest or highest. No other waterfall has so many separate channels – about 275 of them. In the channels are many islands of rock. From what looks like an ocean of river over 4 km wide, the Iguaçu Falls crash 82 m over the horseshoe-shaped rim of the Parana Plateau, into a narrow gorge named La Garganta del Diablo (Devil's Throat), and then spread out into many cascades.

At the height of the rainy season, from November to March, about 13.6 million litres of water – enough to fill six Olympic swimming pools – pour into the Devil's Throat every second. The thunderous noise of the falls in full flood can be heard over 24 km away.

▶ Iguaçu Falls, seen from below on the Argentinian side.

▼ Water crashes down the giant staircase of the Iguaçu Falls on the Brazilian side.

Iguaçu means 'big water' in the language of the local people, who say that the waterfalls were made by a god ripping a gorge in the earth. The falls were first seen by a European in 1541. Unlike almost everyone before or since, Alvar Nuñez Cabeza de Vaca was not especially impressed by the falls, saying only that his party had had to carry their canoes round them.

Crater Lake

Nearly 7,000 years ago, Mount Mazama in Oregon, USA, was a volcano, with glaciers on its side up to 300 m thick and 19 km long. In a huge eruption, about 1,000 m of the top of the mountain was blasted away. Some of the rest of the mountain collapsed into the huge empty chamber from which the lava and ash that formed the volcano had burst out. Water filled up the hole, making what is called a 'caldera' or crater lake.

Crater Lake is about 9.5 km long and 8–9.5 km wide. At 589 m, it is the second deepest lake on the American continent (after Great Slave Lake in Canada) and the seventh deepest in the world. Because the water is very clear, the lake is always deep blue in colour. The water temperature never rises above 13°C, and the lake has only been known to freeze once. Now a new volcanic cone, called Wizard Island, has begun to form in the lake. One pile of lava debris is known as the Phantom Ship because it seems to sail the lake like a ghost.

▶ A waterfall near Crater Lake State Park.

▼ Coniferous forests grace the edge of Oregon's deep-blue Crater Lake.

The local Native Americans used to believe that looking at Crater Lake brought bad luck. According to their legends, the earth gods tore up a mountain and hurled it after their enemy, Llao, the god of the underworld. The peak landed in the ground, forever sealing Llao under the earth, but also making a huge hole, which eventually filled with water to form the lake.

Niagara Falls

The Niagara Falls are thought to be about 10,000 years old, and formed at the end of the last Ice Age. They allow water from Lake Erie to flow down to Lake Ontario, 100 m lower. They are not the highest, widest or largest falls in the world, but they are certainly the most famous. Their power and beauty strike all who see them.

The falls lie on the Niagara River, which divides around Goat Island into the American Falls, 323 m across and 56 m high, and the sweeping semicircle of the Canadian or Horseshoe Falls, which have 94 per cent of the water and are 675 m across and 54 m high. You can walk behind the American Falls to the Cave of the Winds, which has been hollowed out by pounding waters.

▶ The viewing tower offers amazing views of the great sweep of the semicircular Horseshoe Falls.

▼ Probably the most famous and most visited falls in the world, the Falls are around 10,000 years old.

Niagara Falls have been the scene of many accidents, and also of some daredevil stunts. In 1859, the French tightrope walker, Charles Blondin, made a spectacular crossing of the waterfalls on a wire 335 m long and 49 m above the roaring waters.
Later he made other crossings blindfolded, on stilts or carrying his manager on his back.

The Okavango Delta

The Okavango Delta in northern Botswana is the largest inland delta on Earth – when it reaches its full size, the Delta bulges out over 22,000 sq. km.

The Okavango River rises in the highlands of Angola as the Cubango River. In the March heavy rains, it floods south across the border into the Kalahari desert of Botswana. For a distance it travels through a fairly narrow corridor bounded by ridges 15 km apart. The water spills on to the flood plain, breaking through barriers of reeds, swirling around islands and filling dried-up pools and channels.

Thousands of animals flee from the flood water when it arrives, but others come to breed and feed, such as 400 species of birds, tiger fish, crocodiles, hippos, terrapins and toads.

▶ Grasses, shrubs and trees grow in the waters and on the islands of the Okavango swamps.

▼ A boy poles a boat through one of the patches of open water in the Okavango Delta.

The baYei people of the region are hunters who use dugout boats called *mekoro* to travel about over the Delta. They try to avoid direct meetings with hippos, which can overturn their boats easily. Hippos are useful in the Delta because they keep the channels open, both by trampling on plants and by eating a lot of grass.

The Sudd

The Sudd is a swamp on the River Nile in the lowlands of central Sudan about 320 km wide and 400 km long. When it floods, it is the size of Ireland. The region is inhabited by the Nuer people, who raise animals. The 360-km Jonglei or Junqali Canal was built in the 1980s, and is twice as long as the Suez Canal.

It was built not only to provide irrigation for crops and to help increase Egypt's water supply, but also to bypass the Sudd. This is because half the water that flows from the Mountain Nile into the Sudd evaporates or seeps into the ground. The Sudd is a barrier to the movement of people – in the floods, cars and trucks cannot pass the slippery mud.

Wild animals migrate seasonally across the Sudd, especially the tiang, an antelope, but the canal bars their route.

▶ Papyrus beside the River Nile in the Sudan, silhouetted against the sky at sunset.

▼ When the River Nile is in flood, an area the size of Ireland is under water.

The engineer Sir William Garstin reported in 1908 that 'The most barren desert that I have ever crossed is a bright and cheerful locality compared with the ... marshland.' He did not know about the changes brought in the Sudd by the seasons, nor that the local people believe this to be the finest land in the world.

The Pantanal

Between the Bolivian mountains in the west and the uplands of Brazil in the east is one of the widest marshy areas in the world. The Pantanal is a series of vast river plains, stretching about 160 km along the eastern bank of the Paraguay River and covering an area of 100,000 sq. km – about the size of Iceland. Every year, when the Paraguay River floods, the Pantanal becomes an immense swamp, leaving only the tops of some low hills dry.

Between November and March, the Pantanal receives 200–300 mm of rainfall. The floods begin in December, but the water reaches its highest point in June. Many of the animals that live in this region then move south to drier ground. In the water live jacaré (a type of alligator), caymans (a type of crocodile), capybaras (water pigs) and giant otters. Anacondas, up to 6 m long, lurk in the shallows to squeeze their prey to death.

▶ A jacaré (a type of alligator) pokes its head out of the vegetation of the Pantanal swamp.

▼ Cattle graze on the grasslands of the Pantanal during the drier months of the year.

The horned frog of the Pantanal is so called because of a horn-like flap of skin above each eye. Because of its bright colouring and readiness to attack, it is often mistakenly thought to be poisonous. It eats snails, mice and other, smaller frogs, which it swallows with its huge mouth.

The Everglades

The Everglades is a marshy region, about 160 km long by 80–120 km wide, that takes up most of the southern part of the state of Florida in the USA. The Native Americans call the Everglades Pa-hay-okee (River of Grass). Through the region, water moves slowly south from the edge of Lake Okeechobee to Florida Bay.

Much of the area is covered with a reed called saw grass, so called because its edges are lined with tiny sharp teeth. There are many small islands called 'hammocks' on which trees and plants, such as mahogany, palms, ferns, orchids and the oddly named gumbo-limbo tree, grow as thickly as in a jungle.

The Everglades are very rich in wildlife. More than 300 species of birds live here for at least part of each year, especially wading birds, such as ibis, egrets and herons. Large turtles, snakes, tree frogs and manatees are found here, too. The best-known animal is the alligator. Once hunted ruthlessly for its hide, it is now protected by law.

In the nineteenth century, incoming settlers did their best to turn the Everglades into farmland by draining it. Eventually, this was stopped and the region became a national park. However, the survival of the Everglades, and the animals that live there, is at risk from pollution and human greed.

▶ An aerial view of a road and wharf running through the Everglades.

▼ A typical scene in the Everglades or 'River of Grass'.

Red Mangrove Swamps

'No one likes the mangroves,' said the American novelist, John Steinbeck. Yet mangroves are strange and interesting trees that do no harm and some good. They are found on many tropical coasts.

Mangroves like low-lying, muddy shores and grow as high as 30 m. They have tangled, aerial roots that look like spidery legs. The mud and debris that are carried on the tide and get trapped in the roots build up new land. The trees break up storm waves and their roots fix the soil in place, preventing it from being swept away by the sea.

There are red, black, white and buttonwood mangroves. The red mangroves of Florida grow along the southern shoreline of the state and on the thousands of islands offshore. They are also a home for the wildlife.

▲ The crowded trunks of red mangrove trees.

The mangroves grow so thickly and over such a wide area that they make a perfect hiding-place. Some escaped prisoners have managed to survive in the Florida red mangroves for a year before being caught. They are also a good place to shelter from typhoons.

▼ Mangroves grow along low-lying, muddy shores, as here at Rabbit Key, Florida. Such forests are found on many tropical coasts around the world.

Vatnajökull

Vatnajökull is the greatest ice-cap in Iceland, often called the 'land of ice and fire'. This huge sheet of ice covers 8,420 sq. km, about one-twelfth of the country. What makes it unusual is that under the ice, and sometimes cradled in it, are lava flows, volcanic craters and hot lakes.

Iceland is still growing and changing. It sits on the Mid-Atlantic Ridge, a volcanic mountain range mostly under the sea. The Ridge has filled in a long split in the earth's surface caused by the tectonic plates tearing apart. Iceland is just below the Arctic Circle, which is why it has such a cold climate.

On Vatnajökull is a caldera (huge crater) called Grimsvötn, and in it is a hot lake 488 m deep. The lake is covered by some 200 m of ice, but this is heated from below and some of it melts. When ice turns to water it takes up more space. At Grimsvötn, the water volume will eventually burst through the ice. This violent outpouring of water, called 'Jökulhaup' in Icelandic, is so strong that it carries off everything in its path, including chunks of ice over 20 m high.

▶ A glacier and some of the snow fields of Vatnajökull.

▼ Lakes, icebergs and mountains are features of the scenery of Vatnajökull, the greatest ice-cap in Iceland.

In another part of the Vatnajökull are the craggy remains of a volcano called Oraefajökull. In a huge explosion in 1362, it buried or demolished everything for miles around. There was only one survivor, a farmer who heard the first two of the three great crashes of the eruption and took shelter in a cave.

Los Glaciares

Lake Argentino, near the southern tip of the Andes in South America, is the scene of a spectacular natural drama. The lake is fed by glaciers that crawl down the mountains of the high Patagonian ice-cap. There are nine glaciers in this area, called Los Glaciares. Every two or three years, the Moreno Glacier reaches the shore of the lake and keeps on going unmelted until it reaches the opposite shore as a wall of bluish-white ice up to 60 m high.

Lying across the lake like a giant log, the glacier dams the water behind it. Upstream from the ice dam, the water level rises to as much as 37 m above the level below the glacier. The pressure of the dammed water builds up and eventually some seeps under the glacier, hollowing out a huge tunnel. The walls of the tunnel weaken until at last it collapses and a thundering torrent bursts through, with such force that the roar and the ear-splitting cracks can be heard 6 km away.

▶ Ultima Esperanza (Last Hope), a magnificent glacier that sweeps down from the Patagonian ice-cap.

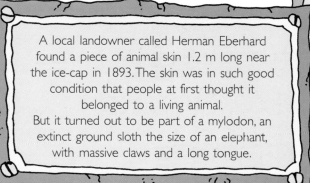

▼ Clouds over the Andes and the lakes of Patagonia.

A local landowner called Herman Eberhard found a piece of animal skin 1.2 m long near the ice-cap in 1893. The skin was in such good condition that people at first thought it belonged to a living animal.

But it turned out to be part of a mylodon, an extinct ground sloth the size of an elephant, with massive claws and a long tongue.

The Ross Ice Shelf

The Ross Ice Shelf is a huge triangular raft of ice almost filling a bay in the Antarctic coast. About 800 km wide and extending about 970 km inland, it is the largest body of floating ice – about the size of France. The shelf was discovered in 1840 by the British captain Sir James Clark Ross on an expedition to locate the South Magnetic Pole. They picked their way through the pack ice and came out into open water, only to meet a vertical ice cliff rising 50–60 m above the sea, impossible to pass through.

Some of the coastline is an unbroken line of cliffs. At others there are bays and headlands. The ice thickness varies from 185 to 760 m. The shelf, like a loosely moored raft, is being pushed out to sea at about 1.5 to 3 m a day, partly by glaciers flowing from the land. Chunks break off and float away as icebergs.

▲ Ice floes break off the Ross Ice Shelf below Mount Erebus (about 3,795 m), the highest mountain of Antarctica and the world's highest active volcano.

The Ross Ice Shelf was the starting-point for both the Norwegian and British expeditions that raced to be first to the South Pole in 1911. Roald Amundsen's party left from the Bay of Whales, while Robert Falcon Scott set off from Ross Island, where the Ice Shelf joins the mainland, nearly 100 km further from the Pole. Amundsen beat Scott to the Pole by a month.

▼ At this point, the cliffs of the Ross Ice Shelf rise about 30 m above the sea.

The Amphitheatre

The Amphitheatre is an enormous semi-circle of flat-topped cliffs in the Royal Natal National Park in South Africa. The cliffs are 1,500 m high, rising at the ends to around 3,000 m. The plateau at the top of the cliffs is called Pofung, which means 'place of the eland' (a type of African deer) in the local language. The Amphitheatre is part of the Drakensberg (Dragon Mountain) range that stretches 1,000 km from the Cape of Good Hope to the Transvaal.

Below the cliffs is one of South Africa's oldest game reserves, Giant's Castle. Eland, antelopes, baboons, eagles and lammergeiers (a type of bird) are just a few of the beasts that can be found there. There are huge cracks in the rock, sometimes running down the full length of the cliffs, and rock bulges that seem like supports holding the cliffs in place.

▲ The great sweep of the Amphitheatre towers over the Giant's Castle Reserve. Geologists have found the fossil bones of dinosaurs and three-toed footprints of another unknown animal there.

The Drakensberg has many wonders, such as the sandstone caves in the lower slopes where there are paintings by the Bushmen, who once hunted using poisoned arrows all over southern Africa. There are over 5,000 paintings in the Giant's Castle Reserve alone.

▼ The Devil's Tooth looms up into the mist from the Amphitheatre.

The Ahaggar Mountains

The Ahaggar (or Hoggar) Mountains of Algeria lie at the heart of the Sahara about 1,500 km south of the city of Algiers. From a rocky plateau about 2,000 m high, they rise to 3,003 m above sea-level at Mount Tahat. The Ahaggar range is made up of rocks 2,000 million years old, and are part of the ancient bedrock of the African continent.

Some of the peaks are volcanic plugs, that is, hardened magma filling the neck of extinct volcanoes. Over the years, the outer layers of the volcanoes were eroded (worn away) by wind and water, leaving just the black plugs standing above the pink granite of the plateau. The tallest of the weirdly-shaped peaks, the Ilamen, is 2,670 m high.

The Ahaggar was controlled by the hardy Tuareg people, who moved from oasis to oasis. Tuareg means 'lost souls' in Arabic. Sometimes called 'the Blue Men of the Sahara', they are famous for their shiny, blue robes, and the veils worn by men – to protect their souls, they say, but also to protect their faces from the wind and sand.

▲ These rock boulders and pinnacles are typical of the landscape of the Ahaggar Mountains, Algeria.

◄ Though very bare, the Ahaggar scenery is very beautiful in the early morning.

The Ruwenzori

The Ruwenzori mountain range was formed about 2 million years ago. It is 125 km long and runs along the Zaire-Uganda border. In the local African language, Ruwenzori means 'rainmaker', and it is, indeed, very rainy and misty, with clouds hiding the mountain peaks on 300 days a year.

Everything here seems to be at least twice its normal size. Earthworms in the Ruwenzori grow up to 1 m long and are as thick as a man's thumb. Black hogs are the giants among Africa's wild pigs, weighing about 160 kg and standing 1 m high at the shoulder. The lobelia, a plant found in many gardens, here becomes a candle-shaped flower spike 2 m high. Mountain bamboo grows to 9–12 m and sedge grasses to 1.8 m. Botanists think

▶ The Ruwenzori are noted for their oversized plants, here seen against the background of Lower Kitandara Lake and Mt Luigi di Savoia (4,626 m).

▼ Climbers on the Elena Glacier (about 4,600 m), one of the permanent snow fields in the Ruwenzori.

One of the strangest creatures living in the Ruwenzori is the three-horned chameleon, which the local people believe brings bad luck. Another unusual animal is the hyrax, a tiny relative of the elephant, which looks like a rabbit but has hoofs instead of claws, and shrieks loudly when greeting a fellow animal or when disturbed or frightened.

that these plants and animals grow to monster size because of the high rainfall, strong sunlight and acid soil.

The Ruwenzori are remarkable also for the fact that, although they are only 48 km north of the equator, their peaks are never without their beautiful, silvery snow caps. The British explorer Henry Morton Stanley was the first European to see them, in 1888, but the Greek geographer Ptolemy (AD 90–168) had written about the 'Mountains of the Moon', which he said were the source of the River Nile. People think he must have meant the Ruwenzori.

Staffa

All around the edge of the small island of Staffa, off the west coast of Scotland, are columns made of basalt. These rocks were pushed up by volcanic movements, about 70 million years ago, and then eroded. The columns are mostly six-sided, and packed tightly together so that they look like the pipes of an organ. Some are about 40 m high.

A tongue of shorter columns leads to Staffa's best-known feature, Fingal's Cave. Fishermen in the Inner Hebrides called it a 'musical cave' because of the harp-like sounds made by air currents blowing around the pillars. Near the entrance to the cave is Fingal's Chair. Anyone who sits there can make three wishes that will be granted, it is said. The entrance is a marvellous archway and the cave itself is like a huge funnel, 60 m long, narrowing from 13 m high at the opening to 6 m at the far end.

Similar columns of basalt, the Giant's Causeway (see page 85), can be found in Northern Ireland. According to Irish legend, this is one end of the road built by the giant, Finn MacCool. The other end, 120 km away, is the island of Staffa.

▼ Fluted cliffs stand like soldiers guarding the entrance to Fingal's Cave on the island of Staffa in the Inner Hebrides.

Staffa has had many famous visitors including Queen Victoria with some of her family in 1847. Artists, poets and composers have produced many excellent works with Staffa in mind. Perhaps the best-loved work is the *Hebrides Overture*, better known as *Fingal's Cave*, written by the German composer Felix Mendelssohn after his visit there in 1829.

The Matterhorn

Edward Whymper, an English mountaineer, led the first successful ascent of the Matterhorn in 1865. That first ascent was a tragic affair. Four of the seven men in the party died when a rope snapped and they plunged down the North Face. The body of one of the climbers was never found.

The Matterhorn is well known for its magnificent outline and its position towering above the Swiss village of Zermatt. It is not the highest mountain in the Alps, nor even the highest peak in Switzerland, but it has four very marked ridges and four faces that give it the shape of a pyramid. Its beauty is made even more striking by the way it stands alone with no other peaks close by.

The Alps were created around 40 million years ago when two sections of the Earth's crust crashed into each other, throwing up rock into a chain of buckled, folded mountains.

▼ The magnificent pyramid shape of the Matterhorn, with its customary plume of cloud near the peak.

One of the most determined guides, Perren, had the nickname 'the wolf of the mountains'. He decided he would not retire until he had climbed the Matterhorn 150 times. However, his strength and skill finally gave out, and he fell to his death. But he had nearly reached his target with 144 successful climbs.

Elburz Mountains

The land and sea borders of Iran are guarded almost everywhere by mountains. The best-known and highest is the great snow cone of Damavand (5,604 m), a slightly active volcano. It is the highest peak in the Elburz mountains, a 900-km range that runs south of the Caspian Sea (see page 41) across northern Iran.

Damavand is often mentioned in Iranian legends and some people say that Noah's ark was stranded here after the Great Flood. The northern side is thickly forested with beech and oak. The southern side, because of the lack of rain (only 280–500 mm a year), is near-desert. The Elburz mountains used to be famous for Hyrcanian tigers, but these are now rare. Snow leopards and lynx are still found there, however.

▶ The Elburz mountains with Damavand at the rear.

▼ Snow on the Elburz mountains near Tehran in Iran.

The deepest cave in Asia is under another range of mountains in south-western Iran. Ghar Parau (571 m deep) lies under the Zagros mountains. It was found and explored in 1971–2 by some British cavers. They found that the only way in was via a 'dreadful, narrow canyon' on the floor of a keyhole-shaped passage which varied between 30 and 180 cm wide.

The Karakoram

The Karakoram is a great range of mountains lying parallel to the Punjab Himalaya, part of the Greater Himalaya. It runs for about 400 km through northern India and Pakistan. Karakoram means 'black rubble' in Turkish – an unlikely name for these glittering, white-capped peaks.

The range has more and longer glaciers than anywhere in the world outside the polar regions. The greatest is the Hispar-Biafo Glacier (100 km long) crossing the Hispar Pass. Rising above them are long avenues of peaks. Among these giants is K2, the second highest mountain in the world at 8,610 m.

It was first climbed in 1954 by an Italian party led by Ardito Desio. It is sometimes called the Savage Mountain because it has claimed many lives.

In all, there are nineteen mountains in the Karakoram above 7,260 m. The peaks usually have sharp, bold shapes with hundreds of towers and spires clustered around them.

▼ The Hunza River on the Chinese-Pakistan border and some of the mountains of the Karakoram, with their typical jagged, snow-capped peaks.

People live in the Karakoram in villages as high as 4,500 m and yak and goat herders wander from pasture to pasture with their animals. Mountaineers from the West have employed the local people as porters on their expeditions. The mountains are home to mountain sheep, antelope, wolves, brown bears and the rare snow leopard.

Mount Everest

The Himalayas were formed in the last few million years. After the supercontinent of Laurasia broke up, India moved slowly north towards Asia and then crashed into it. The sea-bed between the two plates was crumpled and pushed up on the northern rim of India to form mountains. These two plates of the Earth's crust are still moving, so the Himalayas are being pushed still higher.

The highest mountain on the planet, Mount Everest, is growing about 5 cm a year. Satellite technology says the mountain is currently 8,872 m tall. First recognized as the highest peak in 1852, it got its Western name in 1862.

Mount Everest straddles the border between Nepal and Tibet. Near the end of the nineteenth century, Tibet and Nepal closed their borders to Europeans. It was not until the early 1920s that Westerners were allowed to try to climb Everest.

The first-known successful climb was by the New Zealander, Edmund Hillary, and the Sherpa, Tenzing Norgay, in 1953. Since then, Everest has been climbed by about 400 people. Access is restricted by the Nepalese so as to prevent too much damage to the environment.

▼ Everest at sunset, photographed from the south some 40 km away. On the right are its sister peaks, Lhotse and Nuptse, which are both also among the world's highest mountains.

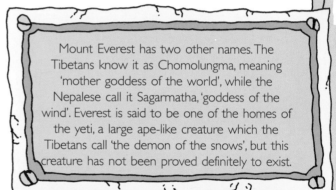

Mount Everest has two other names. The Tibetans know it as Chomolungma, meaning 'mother goddess of the world', while the Nepalese call it Sagarmatha, 'goddess of the wind'. Everest is said to be one of the homes of the yeti, a large ape-like creature which the Tibetans call 'the demon of the snows', but this creature has not been proved definitely to exist.

Chocolate Hills

If you believe the legend of the people of Bohol, an island in the Philippines, the rounded hills that sit in the centre of the island are the tears shed by a giant called Arogo when his beloved, an ordinary girl named Aloya, failed to return his love, sickened and died.

Another local tale is that two angry giants got into a fight in which they threw rocks at each other, until they simply tired of the battle, made friends and left the island together.

These are only stories but, strange to say, we do not know exactly how this cluster of hills was formed. They are made of limestone and may have been produced simply by millions of years of wearing away by the rain. They are unusual because they do not seem to have any of the cave systems or underground passages that are found in most other limestone regions.

The hills – 1,268 of them – are packed closely together like haystacks in a field. Some have domed tops, others are cone shaped. They are covered with rough grass, which is bright green in the rainy season. In the dry season, from February to May, the hot sun dries the grass and turns it the chocolate-brown colour from which the hills get their name.

▼ The famous, but mysteriously formed, Chocolate Hills of the Philippines, photographed in the dry season.

The Philippines are named after King Philip II of Spain. The island of Bohol was where, in 1565, a pact of friendship was agreed between a local chief and a Spaniard sent by Philip. They sealed the treaty by drinking wine mixed with their own blood, which they allowed to dribble into the cup from cuts on their wrists.

Paine Horns

The Andes of South America is a chain of volcanoes made of granite, overlaid with a layer of slate. In places, masses of underground granite were thrown up by movements inside the earth, breaking through the surface crust as pillars. Glaciers then eroded these pillars, leaving them curved on top and with very steep, sometimes upright, sides.

This is how the Paine (pronounced PIE-NAY) Horns, in southern Chile, came to be made. They are two peaks of pinkish-grey granite tipped with black slate, overlooking rolling grassland, bogs with carpets of red, yellow and green mosses, and lakes of motionless, crystal-clear water. Each peak stands only about 2,545 m high, but what makes them so stunning is that they tower like skyscrapers above the surrounding land.

▶ The Towers in the Torres del Paine National Park, Patagonia, Chile.

▼ Snow-capped peaks of the Cerro Paine Grande.

The weather in the Cordillera del Paine is often dreadful, so that mountaineers often find the conditions right on only a few days each season. In 1974, a South African team took six weeks to climb the 1,220-m East Face of the Central Tower of the sheer-sided peaks, the Paine Towers. This was then the highest rock-face to have been climbed.

Mount Roraima

The highlands of Venezuela and the countries to the east form a great semicircle of mesas on the northern side of Amazonia (see page 98). At the point where the borders of three countries meet – Venezuela, Brazil and Guyana – is the largest of the mesas, called Mount Roraima. 2,810 m high, it rises from the plain like the prow of a great ship.

The tableland is about 300 million years old and was originally the bottom of vast, shallow lakes and deltas, forced upwards by movements of the Earth and eroded into mountains and rocky outcrops. In places, the marks left by ripples of water have been preserved in the rock and can be seen on top of the mesa. Roraima is a local name meaning 'mother of streams' and from here the heavy rain runs off to feed rivers in all three neighbouring countries.

▲ Part of the summit of a high tableland surrounded by swirling mist, in the Guayana highlands, Venezuela.

The south-west wall of Roraima is about 6.2 km long and ends at Towashing Pinnacle. It was on this part of the mountain that Sir Arthur Conan Doyle set his story *The Lost World* (written in 1912), which was inhabited by pterodactyls and other prehistoric monsters.

▼ Clouds hide part of the south-west wall of Mount Roraima.

Monument Valley

Imagine a pair of mittens, pointing upwards, hundreds of feet high and made of rust-coloured stone. This is one of the many wonderful formations in Monument Valley, on the border between the states of Utah and Arizona in the USA. About 250 million years ago, the area was covered in sandstone, over which lay a shallow sea. Mud was laid down, which gradually turned to shale. Slowly the water dried up and then, about 70 million years ago, the Earth's crust moved up violently. Since then, the layers of rock have been worn away by wind and rain, leaving dozens of spires, towers, tablelands and broad buttes standing alone.

Like most of the South-west, Monument Valley is very beautiful, but not an easy place for plants or animals to live. It is very dry, with usually less than 200 mm of rain a year. Almost the only plants are shrubs and cacti that can survive without water for months, but sudden rains can bring wild flowers into short but brilliant life.

▶ This aerial view shows the rocks' shadows stretching for many kilometres across the valley floor.

▼ These formations are well named The Mittens.

The American film director, John Ford, used Monument Valley as a setting for over twenty-five westerns in the 1920s and 1930s. Gouldings Trading Post was set up in 1923, but the dining-room was especially built for Ford's film about the US cavalry, called *She Wore a Yellow Ribbon*.

Mammoth and Flint Ridge Caves

The largest cave system in the world is in the USA, under the Mammoth Cave National Park, about 144 km south of the town of Louisville in Kentucky. The caves were first entered by Europeans in 1799. In 1972, cave explorers showed that the cave passages beneath three ridges – the Flint, Mammoth Cave and Toohey – are joined together making a system at least 560 km long.

The caves were formed by water dissolving limestone underneath a layer of hard rocks. The astonishing collection of stalactites and stalagmites forms curtains and waterfalls of solid limestone, and delicate crystals that look like flowers.

Echo River, 110 m underground, shelters various types of fish, crayfish and shrimps. Living things change over the years to suit their environment, and so in a totally dark river they have all evolved to be blind and colourless.

▲ Mammoth Cave has an astonishing collection of formations called stalactites (hanging from the ceiling) and stalagmites (rising from the ground).

Explorers have found the bodies of Native Americans in the caves. These have been preserved (the flesh has not rotted away) partly because they have been wrapped up in cloths like Egyptian mummies and partly because the temperature in the caves is always a cool 12°C.

Eisriesenwelt

South of Salzburg, Austria, perched 1,000 m above the valley floor is the entrance to Eisriesenwelt (World of the Ice Giants), a cave system stretching at least 40 km into the Tennen mountains.

Almost the first thing that can be seen on entering is an ice wall, 30 m high and topped by a maze of caverns and passageways. Throughout this wonderland of beautiful, delicately coloured formations, are shapes like curtains, statues, cascades, needles, columns and flowers. Unlike in many other caves, where the shapes are made of limestone, here they are made of ice.

Eisriesenwelt is the largest cave system in Austria and probably the largest series of permanently ice-filled caves anywhere in the world. The temperature in the caves stays at about

In 1879, the first explorer of the caves went about 200 m into the mountain and found the wall of ice, but thought he could go no further. The main caves were found in 1912–13. An urn holding the ashes of the leader of the first proper explorations stands in the cavern named after him: Alexander von Moerk's Cathedral.

freezing all year round, so when water drips in through cracks and holes in the ceilings, it becomes solid straight away.

The caves were formed over 2 million years ago, when the climate in Europe was much warmer than now. Water flowing over and into the limestone rock gradually dissolved the rock and left this huge and complicated underground region of passages and chambers.

◀ An ice spire rises out of the ice-covered floor of a passageway at Eisriesenwelt.

Frasassi Caves

The 3.2-km long Frasassi Gorge at Ancona in Italy, was carved by the rapidly flowing River Sentino on its north-eastern course from the Apennine Mountains to the sea. It has steep limestone walls pockmarked with cave openings. In 1971, an extraordinary 13-km network of caverns and passages was discovered by a team of cave scientists exploring the area.

   Called Grotta Grande del Vento (Great Cave of the Wind), the system stretches under the Apennines. The team were astonished to find a superb display of still, clear pools, mud banks and caves with limestone shapes that look like frosted crystal. Some formations look like lace curtains, delicate flowers or candles. Some are almost transparent, others are all the colours of the rainbow.

▶ ▼ A wonderful array of columns, stalactites, stalagmites and other limestone shapes are to be found in the caverns of the Frasassi Caves.

It is dark in the caves and there is not much for creatures to eat, but flatworms, millipedes, crayfish and blind cave salamanders (amphibians related to newts) live happily here. Most plentiful are the bats, nocturnal mammals that come out by night to feed and roost by day in La Grotta del Nottole (Cave of the Bats).

The Mulu Caves

The Gunung Mulu National Park is an area of very rich tropical rainforest in north-eastern Sarawak (a state of Malaysia on the island of Borneo). Mulu probably contains more cave by volume than anywhere else in the world, with longer and higher passages, deeper shafts and 'more cubic feet of limestone missing' (as one scientist put it) than had been seen before.

All the caves were formed by running water, some as long ago as 5 million years. The largest known cavern in the world is here – the Sarawak Chamber or Lobang Nasip Bagus, which is 700 m long, 300 m wide and 70 m high. It is big enough to garage 7,500 buses.

Deer Cave, so called because the hard-packed earth at the entrance is pitted with deer footprints, is also enormous – 174 m wide and 120 m high – large enough to hold St Paul's Cathedral in London five times over.

▲ A strangely shaped limestone formation in the Langwaki caves at Mulu.

▼ Stalagmites seem to support the gently arched roof of Lubang Angin cave in Mulu National Park.

An astonishing variety of wildlife is found in the caves. Bats roost in them and the smell of their guano (droppings) fills the air. Huntsman spiders are plentiful, preying on crickets that have antennae 46 cm long. There are also hairy earwigs, eyeless white crabs, swiftlets in their thousands, and black-and-white-striped snakes up to 2.5 m long.

The Glow-worms of Waitomo Cave

The New Zealand glow-worm is the larva of a type of gnat that likes to live in dark, damp places. To attract food, the larvae can make their tails emit light. The larvae sit inside a kind of web and let down sticky threads into water. Midges, attracted to the light, become trapped in these threads and the glow-worms can then pull them up and feed.

The best place to see these larvae is Glow-worm Grotto, in Waitomo Cave, one of many limestone caves in New Zealand's North Island. A river flows into the caves, and about 18 m above its entrance is an opening in the hillside. Following a passage sparkling with stalactites and stalagmites, you reach an underground lake in a large cavern 15 m high. Here a boat takes you into the heart of the cave where the artificial lights are turned off. As your eyes get used to the dark, you can see more and more until it looks as if the whole cave is glowing. You can read your watch by the glow.

▶ Adventurous tourists can go 'black rafting' in the cave.

▼ Thousands of glow-worms make an extraordinary glow across the whole ceiling of Waitomo Cave.

Waitomo is the name given to the cave by the Maoris of New Zealand. It means 'water going in'. They believed that fierce dragons lived in the caves and so were frightened to go inside. Visits only started after the river had been explored by raft in the nineteenth century.

The Great Rift Valley

More than 1,000 million years ago there was one huge supercontinent, which broke up and the plates, or sections, started to drift apart, making the continents we know today. They are still drifting apart. The eastern fringe of Africa is moving eastwards along with Asia, while the rest of Africa is drifting gently to the west. This is thought to result in huge parallel cracks called rifts, which cause the middle section of rock to slip down to produce a deep 'valley' with high cliffs on either side.

The Great Rift Valley or East African Rift Valley is a series of massive trenches, 6,400 km long and mostly between 40 and 56 km wide. It starts in the Taurus Mountains in Turkey and stretches south through Jordan, along the Dead Sea and part of the Red Sea,

into Ethiopia, through Kenya and Tanzania, and on down to Mozambique. A western branch arches round through Uganda, Zaire and Malawi. In this part is Lake Tanganyika, the second deepest lake in the world at 1,436 m, and several other large lakes. The beds of some of the lakes are a long way below sea-level.

The walls of the Great Rift Valley are mostly 600–900 m above the valley floor, but in some places more than 2,700 m. There are several volcanoes along the rift, including Mt Kilimanjaro, 5,895 m high, and Mt Kenya, 5,199 m.

The lakes and walls of the Great Rift Valley form the borders of many East African countries. Ethiopia is skirted by parts of the Great Rift Valley, which have always protected it from invasion, like the moat and walls of a castle.

▼ The cone and crater of Mt Meru (4,565 m) rise up from the floor of the Great Rift Valley. In the clouds in the background is Mt Kilimanjaro.

Fossils have been found on the shores of Lake Turkana, Kenya, and in the Olduvai Gorge, Tanzania, which show that human-like creatures lived there well over 3 million years ago. Some scientists think that the Great Rift Valley is where humans first evolved.

The Fjords of Norway

During the last Ice Age, Norway was covered with mighty glaciers. These ice rivers moved slowly to the sea, scraping away the rock to produce steep-sided, immensely deep, U-shaped valleys. A fjord is often only 18 m or so deep at its mouth, but near the head of the valley it may be ten times deeper.

When the ice melted about 10,000 years ago, the sea filled up the valleys, which the Norwegians named 'fjords'. There are fjords in Canada, New Zealand and Chile, but the greatest are in Norway. The west coast is slashed by these long, narrow, sea-filled channels. The fjords are very beautiful, although also bleak, lonely and threatening.

▼ The fjords of Norway were formed by glaciers gouging out deep, U-shaped valleys as they slid towards the sea.

Geirangerfjord (above) is one of the most beautiful and mysterious of the Norwegian fjords. Streaming into it down sheer rock walls are many waterfalls, such as the Bridal Veil and the Seven Sisters. At its head is the village of Geiranger, reached only by a road that twists 1,000 m down the mountainside.

Yangzi Gorges

The Yangzi (or Yangtze) is the longest river in China and the third longest in the world. The Chinese call it Chang jiang (Long River). It rises in Tibet and flows into the East China Sea at Shanghai, 6,300 km away. Along the way it passes through some spectacular gorges between the towns of Chongqing and Wuhan. To see them, a three-day and two-night journey along the yellowish river is necessary.

The first gorge at the Chongqing end is called Qutang and is 8 km long. In caves high up in the steep rocks, warriors used to be buried along with their weapons and armour. Vertical walls squeeze the river into a narrow trough. The river then makes a sharp zigzag and turns into Wuxia (Witches) Gorge, nearly 48 km long. The last of the main gorges, Xiling, is 80 km long and contains several smaller gorges. Sailing junks used to be used on the river, but one in ten was badly damaged on any voyage and one in twenty totally wrecked.

▶ Spectacular cliffs border the Yangzi Gorges.

▼ Looking down the Yangzi River where the mountains slope steeply into the water.

In the rainy season, the river often rises by 30 m, sometimes even twice that amount. Quick floods, called 'freshets', can make the waters rise as much as 15–18 m in a single day. So much water builds up in the bottleneck at the end of the gorge that boatmen cannot pass. In 1931, the Yangzi rose so much that it flooded an area the size of Scotland.

Milford Sound

Milford Sound, in the South Island of New Zealand, reaches inland for 20 km. It is a magically beautiful place of soaring cliffs, hanging valleys, waterfalls, thick forest and green water, where the mists and sun make gleaming rainbows and a kaleidoscope of light and shade.

The area is very wet, with rain falling one or two days in every three. In one day, 560 mm of rain once fell. The heavy rain produces thundering waterfalls that tumble 300 m or more into the inlet.

The cliffs are the tallest sea cliffs in the world, rising 1,584 m out of the water and sinking to 400 m below it. Milford Sound is a fjord, carved out by a glacier creeping towards the sea about 20,000 years ago, during the last Ice Age. As in most fjords, the water is shallow at the mouth and deep at the head.

▶ A ferry on Milford Sound is dwarfed by huge, mist-shrouded cliffs.

▼ Mitre Peak is one of the most famous of the mountains that soar above Milford Sound.

The water lies in three layers in the Sound. The surface layer, about 3 m deep, is low in salt because it comes from fresh water flowing over rich soils, so that it turns brownish. This stops much light from getting through.

At the bottom is sea water. In between is a brackish (slightly salty) layer formed by the movement of the top level to the sea.

Colca Canyon and the Valley of the Volcanoes

Colca Canyon, in Peru, in the Andes mountains, looks like a cut in the mountains made by a gigantic knife. It is the world's deepest gorge. The snowy white peaks, often hidden in the clouds, rise 3.2 km above the valley. The Colca River, wild and muddy in the wet season, winds between extinct volcanoes scattered along the valley floor.

Over the mountains from Colca Canyon is the 64-km long Valley of the Volcanoes, where there are 86 cone-shaped volcanoes, some nearly 300 m high. Some of them rise from the fields, others have solid black lava drifting around their feet. Cacti and puya plants grow on some of the cones. Between the Valley of the Volcanoes and the Pacific Ocean is a hot, sandy gully called Toro Muerto, filled with white boulders.

▲ The sides of the Colca Canyon plunge 3,000 m here to the valley floor where the Colca River flows.

▼ Sarancaya volcano, in the Valley of Volcanoes, erupts daily, sending out ash and steam.

Scattered in Toro Muerto are thousands of white boulders with carvings of discs to represent the sun, geometric shapes, snakes, llamas and people wearing strange headgear that looks like space helmets. Nobody knows who engraved them or what they mean. The people are probably not spacemen, although this theory is believed by many.

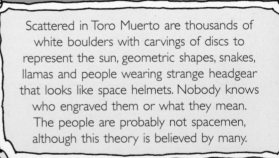

Death Valley

Death Valley is a deep gutter of desert that runs through south-eastern California, USA. It is the hottest and driest place in North America, and its lowest point, 82 m below sea-level, is the deepest area in the whole Americas. It is also very beautiful, with minerals in the rocks glinting like rainbows in the sun.

Death Valley is 225 km long and 8–24 km wide. The valley itself is 1 million years old. About 50,000 years ago, a body of water called Lake Manly filled the valley. More recently, between about 5,000 and 2,000 years ago, a shallow lake could be found here. When the water of this lake evaporated, it left behind a layer of salt in the lowest part of the lake to form the saltpan we see today. Now when water finds its way into the desert, it evaporates so that none drains out.

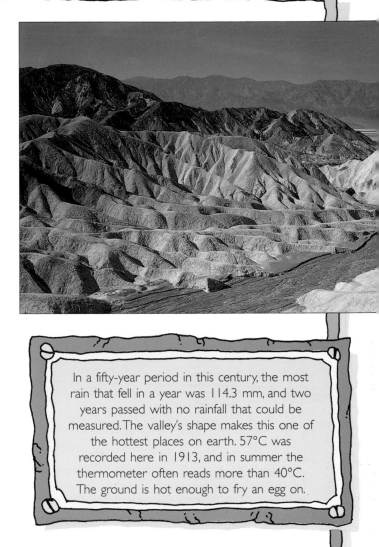

▶ Death Valley from Zabriskie Point.

▼ These mounds resemble holes and bunkers, hence the name of Devil's Golf-course for this area.

In a fifty-year period in this century, the most rain that fell in a year was 114.3 mm, and two years passed with no rainfall that could be measured. The valley's shape makes this one of the hottest places on earth. 57°C was recorded here in 1913, and in summer the thermometer often reads more than 40°C. The ground is hot enough to fry an egg on.

The Grand Canyon

Of all the natural wonders on earth, the Grand Canyon is one of the most splendidly majestic. To stand at its rim and marvel at its staggering vastness and beauty is one of the great experiences in life. The canyon is about 443 km long, plunges 1.6 km to its deepest point, Granite Gorge, and varies in width from 200 m to 29 km.

The Grand Canyon was carved out of a plateau in the north-western part of the state of Arizona that was once the floor of an ancient ocean. Two rivers, the Ancestral (ancient) Colorado and the Hualapai, cut into the plateau until they met and joined to make the modern Colorado River.

At the same time – about 60 million years ago – the plateau was raised upwards by movements within the Earth. The Colorado River was fast-flowing (at up to 32 kph), and washed away the canyon's sides while eroding a deep channel for itself.

The canyon's rocks present a picture in stone of geological history. The youngest rocks, at the top of the canyon, are 225 million years old. Those at the bottom are over 2,000 million years old. All the layers of rock contain fossils of sea beasts, trees and dinosaurs.

The summer temperature on the canyon floor may be 6–7°C higher than on the rim. Rattlesnakes, chuckwallas (a kind of lizard), skunks and scorpions thrive in the desert environment. In the forests and shrubland on the canyon edges live bobcats, porcupines, mule deer, chipmunks and coyote. Mountain lions, though rare, still roam the rocks.

▼ The Grand Canyon, with its multicoloured cliffs, dropping in places 1.6 km to the Colorado River, is one of the most awesome sights in the world.

The Tsingy Lands

At the northern tip of Madagascar is an area of razor-sharp needles of rock called tsingy. The local people, the Malagasy, gave them this name because of the dull, clanging sound that the rocks make if you hit them – a sort of 'tsingy' sound. It is said that, because the needles are so close together, you cannot put one foot down flat on level ground anywhere.

The rocks in the tsingy lands are so viciously sharp and jagged that walking on them will quickly rip the toughest boots to ribbons. If you miss your step, you could scrape all the skin off your leg, or cut an arm or a leg right through to the bone.

The rocks are limestone. Over the years, the heavy rains have eroded the softer rocks, leaving only the hard needles standing. Water seeping through layers of rock forms underground streams, which have hollowed out caverns and channels deep beneath the surface.

One of the biggest caverns is the Grotte d'Andrafiabe, in which about 11 km of passages have been explored so far. The world's only cave-living crocodiles live in these caves for part of the year.

▶ The strange volcanic formations are perfectly reflected in the crystal clear lake at Bemaraha.

▼ Limestone pinnacles in the Tsingy at Bemaraha.

Madagascar is the world's fourth largest island. It split away from the east coast of Africa over 40 million years ago. As a result of its isolation, many of the island's animals are unique. For example, it is the only place in the world where true lemurs live and, out of 250 species of bird that live on the island, more than a hundred are only found on Madagascar.

Balancing Rocks of the Matopo Hills

In the south-west of Zimbabwe, south of Bulawayo, are the Matopo Hills, where, stacked at crazy angles, are natural towers of balancing rocks. These are made of granite – a rock that spewed out of the ground as lava and cooled and solidified to make huge dome-shaped hills.

While this was happening, more than 3,300 million years ago, cracks developed in the granite, and when they were later exposed to the rain and wind, the cracks became larger. At the same time, the outside 'shell' of the rocks began to break away in huge slabs. The result in some cases is large, 'whale-backed' hills; in others, balanced rocks that look as if a light gust of wind would make them fall, yet they have stood for thousands of years. The caves in this wild and difficult country contain some beautiful drawings by the Bushmen.

▶ The touchingly named Mother and Child Rock.

▼ This huge balanced boulder at Domboshawa, Zimbabwe, looks as if it might fall at any moment, but has probably been there for thousands of years.

In this part of Africa there are over a hundred sites where very old granite buildings have been found. The most impressive is the eleventh-century citadel (strong castle) of Great Zimbabwe, to the east of the Matopo Hills. Perhaps the builders of these cities got their ideas from the extraordinary natural features they saw around them.

The Giant's Causeway

The Giant's Causeway is a promontory (tongue) of land on the north-west coast of Co. Antrim, Northern Ireland, made up of columns stretching from the cliff face to the sea. The columns are so regular that they look human-made, but they are wholly natural and are a type of rock called basalt. There are about 37,000 columns, mostly with six sides, and 37–51 cm across. Some are 6 m high. The causeway is 12 m wide in places and is highest where it is narrowest.

About 50–60 million years ago, lava was pushed up through cracks in the ground and flowed as rivers to the sea. This cooled the lava so quickly that it became solid and cracked into large columns. Different formations have names that describe their appearance, such as the Chimney Pots, the Punchbowl and My Lady's Fan. (See also Staffa, page 62.)

▶ The basalt columns are sometimes very regularly shaped and of similar widths and heights.

▼ Some columns have been worn by wind and water into smoother shapes, but you can clearly see six sides on many of them.

In the next bay to the Giant's Causeway, Port na Spaniagh, a ship of the Spanish Armada called the *Girona* was wrecked in 1588, and all except five of its 1,300 crew were drowned. The wreck was excavated in 1967 by a Belgian team of divers who found many coins and other treasures.

Metéora

For more than a thousand years, monks have been living in peace and solitude in monasteries on top of some stunningly beautiful rock pinnacles in the Pindhos mountains of northern Greece. Sixty million years ago, the region was a rocky sea-bed. Then it was thrust upwards by violent earth movements, cracking and splitting as it rose.

The rocks of this place, now called Metéora, were slowly eroded by water, wind, heating and freezing, leaving behind twenty-four massive columns. Horizontal marks on their sides are thought to have been made by waves in ancient times. Some rise up to 550 m above the plain, as high as the CN Tower in Toronto, Canada. Metéora has been called 'the rocky forest of Greece'.

▶ Monasteries and retreats have been built on top of some of these extraordinary rock pinnacles.

▼ The rock pillars of Metéora, shown here at dusk, tower over the valley.

The only way up to the monasteries in early times was by a long ladder, later replaced by a net-and-rope device. Being hauled up was a terrifying experience for anyone not used to being swung to and fro and tipped this way and that over a great abyss. Nowadays steps carved out of the rock lead to the top of some of the pinnacles.

Cappadocia

The region of Cappadocia in central Turkey was made by volcanoes and erosion. Eruptions laid down layers of ash, lava and stones, making a platform 300 m above the neighbouring land. Over ages, the ash was squeezed until it became a soft, pale rock called tufa. The lava on top hardened into black basalt.

Streams, floods and frosts cracked the rocks and wore away the softer parts. What remains is a strange moon-like landscape of cones, pyramids and pinnacles known as 'fairy chimneys'. Many of these weird shapes are striped horizontally in white, ochre, chestnut, red and black. Early in the Christian period, people started to carve hundreds of rock churches and living spaces out of the soft tufa. Some of the cones have so many windows that they look like chunks of Swiss cheese.

▲ People cut windows and doors out of the rock to make a church but the little turret on top is an entirely natural formation.

▼ The tufa has been eroded into these formations, which look like a procession of ghosts.

In the Tokali Kilise (Church with the Shield) in Goreme in central Turkey, tenth-century wall paintings show Jesus and his disciples. Not far away, in the Gorgoli valley, are monasteries and even towns that have been built in caves, carved from rock, or dug underground. The towns were often connected by tunnels several kilometres long and had a maze of passages.

Guilin

Guilin has been called 'the most beautiful landscape under heaven'. It is in a remote area of China, in Guanxi province, near the Vietnam border.

The limestone here is 300 million years old and has been shaped by the action of water into fantastic shapes. Some of the underground streams come out of the sides of mountains in waterfalls. Mists drifting across the mountains make the scenery look like a typical Chinese landscape painting.

Between Guilin and Yang Shuo is a stunning 80-km stretch of the River Li, which flows into the Pearl River. The water itself is full of whirlpools and rapids. Alongside are hills, covered with creepers, some rising straight from the water. The hills are not especially high, but they seem so because they are so steep-sided.

▶ Mountains and rice paddy fields at Guilin.

▼ Boats on the River Li at dusk, Guilin.

The Luditong (Reed Flute Cave) was used for hundreds of years as a hiding-place in troubled times. Dragon Cave is named for the markings on its roof, which look like a dragon trying to escape. It is full of tablets on which are written the names of visitors, some going back 800 years. Another famous cavern is Wind Cave, in the side of Folded Silk Hill.

The Stone Forest

The Stone Forest of Lunan was an area with a solid bed of limestone, which was lifted by earth movements, cracked and the stone partly dissolved and washed away by water. The forest of stone pillars covers an area of about 5 sq. km about 120 km south-east of the city of Kunming in the Chinese province of Yunnan.

Some of the rock formations are certainly like trees, but others are like swords, birds, animals, mushrooms, temples and mountains. Many have names, for example Lotus Blossom Peak, Layered Waterfall, Lion Arbour and Phoenix Preening its Feathers. Some form natural bridges and arches. The shortest of the columns are about as tall as a person and the tallest are 30 m high – about the height of an eight-storey building.

In between the rocks are pools and passages, some with trees and shrubs. Red, pink and purple rhododendrons and camellias grow wild nearby.

▶ The limestone columns seem to form an avenue.

▼ Flowers and shrubs line the passages between the 'trees' of the Lunan Stone Forest.

In June every year the Yi people of this part of China hold a Torch Festival. In one dance, a tiger (two men dressed up) threatens women fruit-pickers and is chased away by men with pitchforks.

Rainbow Bridge

Rainbow Bridge is not only the largest known natural bridge in the world, but it is also one of the most perfectly formed and coloured works of nature anywhere. It arches across a canyon in the red rock desert country in the state of Utah in the USA.

The top of the bridge is an almost perfect quarter circle, reaching up and out from the rim of the sheer cliff that forms one side of the gorge. On the other side, it curves gradually down to meet the canyon floor. The underside is smooth and curved like a cup handle.

This graceful, elegant bridge is 94 m long and spans a canyon 85 m wide. The top is 10 m across – wide enough for a road. It is 88 m from the base to the top – nearly three times the height of Nelson's Column in Trafalgar Square, London, or tall enough for the Capitol in Washington, DC, to fit under it.

The Navajo people who lived in this area also called this magnificent formation 'rainbow bridge', both for its shape and for its wonderful pink and lavender colours, which change shade in the late afternoon sun to red and brown. They believed it was actually a rainbow turned to stone. As rainbows were guardians of the universe, they treated the bridge as a sacred place.

Until 1963 the only way to get to Rainbow Bridge was by a rough overland trail 20 km long. Then the Glen Canyon Dam was built, raising the level of the Colorado River and filling the ninety-one canyons that run into it with water. You can now travel by boat to within a few feet of the great bridge.

▼ Rainbow Bridge, the largest known natural bridge in the world, arches elegantly over the Colorado River.

Bryce Canyon

Bryce Canyon is not actually a canyon – it was not carved out by a river – but the jagged, semicircular eastern end of the Pansaugunt Plateau in Utah, USA.

Southern Utah is like a giant staircase, with Bryce Canyon at the top 2,800 m above sea-level – the lowest step is on the edge of the Grand Canyon. The local Paiute people called the area 'red rocks standing like men in a bowl-shaped canyon'.

Nearly 60 million years ago, the area was covered by water, which laid down a 600-m layer of silt, sand and lime. Then movements of the Earth pushed the land up. The waters drained away and huge beds of rock cracked into blocks as they rose. Then erosion ate into the rock layers and chiselled them into fantastic, craggy shapes. Metals give the towers their wonderful colours.

► A tree reaches up to the light between pinnacles.

▼ Wind and water carved this amazing landscape.

Bryce Canyon is named after a Scottish settler called Ebenezer Bryce, who built a cattle ranch at the foot of the canyon in 1875. It was not an easy area to live and work in. He said the canyon was 'a hell of a place to lose a cow'.

The Arches

The Arches National Park in Utah, USA, contains more natural arches than anywhere else in the world. An arch must be at least 1 m wide. There are more than 1,000 here, plus 'windows', which will in time turn into arches. There are cave-like structures too, and heaps of rubble that once were arches. Ribbon Arch is 15 m long and now is only 6 cm wide and 30 cm deep at its narrowest point, so it will soon collapse.

The area was once a basin below sea-level. About 300 million years ago, it was flooded with seawater, which laid down a layer of salt. Then rocks and other material collected on top to a depth of 1.6 km. The weight made both the salt and the rocks crack and collapse in places. Water then seeped in and eroded away the softer rocks.

▶ The arches were formed by wind erosion and temperature changes, which caused cracking.

▼ Landscape Arch is the longest single arch in the world, 89 m long and 32 m high.

The ground is too bare for anything much to be grown here. John Wesley Wolfe, who had fought and been wounded in the American Civil War of the 1860s, built a ranch here in 1888 and, helped by his son, raised cattle here for twenty years. Visitors can still see their simple cabin and the fenced area for cattle called a corral.

Ayers Rock

This golden-red rock in the Northern Territory of Australia is an 'inselberg', or island mountain. Formed about 500 million years ago from layers of soft sands laid down on the bed of the ocean that once filled central Australia, it was pushed up by movements of the Earth's crust. Most of the rock is underground.

The sandstone of Ayers Rock is rich in feldspar, which looks reddish. It is famous for the way it changes colour, from orange to amber to crimson, with the changing light of the day. Over the years, wind and water have worn the rock away. Today, the flattened top is 348 m above the ground, the base is about 9 km round. The Rock is covered in grooves caused by water running down the surface and eroding rocks of different hardness at different rates.

▶ Maggie Springs, one of the rivulets that runs down the side of Ayers Rock.

▼ Ayers Rock is particularly famous for the way in which it changes colour at different times of day.

The Aboriginals (native Australians) who live in the area call it Uluru, and to them it has always been a sacred place, of which every part has a special meaning. Since 1985, Ayers Rock (named after Sir Henry Ayers, then premier of South Australia) has been returned to the Aboriginals to look after, as part of the Uluru National Park.

The Olgas

The Olgas of central Australia seem to spring up out of nowhere, like rocky red islands rising from a hazy sea. They are 'inselbergs' or island mountains. Originally, they were only pieces of rock under the sea. Gradually, they were pounded into pebbles and boulders, with sand cementing them together. About 500 million years ago, the Earth's movements lifted the rocks above the sea, at the same time tilting them sideways. The wind and water eroded them into the dome shapes we see today.

The highest of the thirty-six domes is Mount Olga. It rises 550 m vertically above the plain to almost twice the height of the Eiffel Tower in Paris, France. Many of the other domes are a lot higher than the lone rock-mountain, Ayers Rock, 32 km away to the east.

▶ The only section of the Olgas open to the public.

▼ It is easy to see why the Aboriginals call the Olgas Kata Tjuta, or 'mountain with many heads'.

According to the legends of the local Aboriginal tribe, the Olgas were made in the 'Dreamtime', before history began, when the gods walked on the Earth and shaped its landscape. They also say that a serpent blows into the Valley of the Winds to make a breeze, and will blow a hurricane to punish wrongdoers.

The Pinnacles

In the seventeenth century, Dutch sailors travelling between Europe and the East Indies, where they were trading in spices, were the first Europeans to see and chart the coast of Australia. Dutch maps showed a desert of sand dunes in an area that is now Nambung National Park, Western Australia. They thought that the strange stone shapes on the dunes were the ruins of cities.

In fact, the Pinnacles were formed entirely by nature. There are many thousands of limestone pillars – some are like needles, others more like stone stacks, with blunt or rounded tops. The tallest are 5 m high and the widest are up to 2 m wide. Scientists thought that they were the remains of a woodland turned to stone, but they now agree that they were formed from wind-blown sand.

▶ These pillars have been worn down by wind and water. Some have toppled over under their weight.

▼ The rows and rows of stone stacks look like the gravestones of a huge cemetery.

Dotted among the Pinnacles are hundreds of objects that look like pencils or small twigs. These are not stones, but the roots of fossilized plants called rhizoliths. Also found in the dunes are fossils that look like eggs, but are actually the pupa cases of a type of weevil. Often you can see the hole at one end where the grown beetle has crawled out.

Wave Rock

Near the town of Hyden, on the edge of the grain-growing region that stretches across Western Australia, is a huge rock formation called Hyden Rock. At its northern end is an overhanging rock called Wave Rock, towering 15 m over the plain. It is so named because it is shaped like a gigantic frozen wave about to break. It is about 100 m long.

Although it stands on bare, dry land, the rock was probably once partly buried (about 2,700 million years ago). Water seeping through the ground had eroded away the underside of the straight-sided rock.

Later the surrounding soil was washed away and then the wind took over shaping the rock, blowing sand and dust into it and scooping out the lower surface, leaving the top curling over. Minerals and chemicals washed down the rock by the rain have left streaks of reddish-brown, black, yellow and grey. The colours are especially bright in the morning sun.

Another beautiful rock near Wave Rock is known as Hippo's Yawn. It is a hollow rock that looks like a hippo's mouth. A few kilometres to the north is another strange group of knobbly rocks called the Humps.

This area of Western Australia is also famous for its gold. Many thousands of people hoping to make their fortunes came here in the 1880s and 1890s to dig for gold. The rush moved elsewhere then, but gold is still mined here in both old and newly opened mines.

▼ Wave Rock looks more like a wave than a rock. It is about 100 m long and 15 m high.

The Bungle Bungles

The Bungle Bungles look like a jumble of giant beehives, striped black and orange as bees are themselves. They are part of a plateau 200 m high, that was once the floor of an ocean that covered this area of Western Australia. The rocks are made of sandstone, a soft rock that crumbles easily. The rugged shapes of the Bungle Bungles are protected by outer 'skins' of black metal silica and orange algae. As soon as this outer layer is damaged, the rock underneath starts to break up and is washed away by rain.

The Bungle Bungles are about 350 million years old. They have been known to the Aboriginals for as long as they have been around – about 24,000 years. There are ancient Aboriginal carvings on some of the rock faces, and the range is a sacred place for them.

▼ The Bungle Bungles are now a national park. Tourists are allowed in, but it is easy to see why four-wheel-drive vehicles are necessary.

Travelling in the Bungle Bungles can be quite an ordeal. The mountainsides are very steep and it is easy to slip on the loose rock that often breaks away at a touch. Heavy summer rainfall causes the rivers to flood and fill up the gorges. Daytime temperatures often reach a searing 50°C. There are tree snakes called night tigers that may bite if cornered or disturbed.

The Amazon Rainforest

Rainforests are found in tropical areas, fairly near to the equator. The heavy rainfall makes the forest grow especially thickly. The Amazon rainforest, the largest in the world, is bigger than Europe, covering 7 million sq. km, and stretching from the lower slopes of the Andes to the Atlantic coast of Brazil.

The Amazon rainforest is vital to the health of the world and everything that lives in it. Trees take in the greenhouse gas, carbon dioxide, which in large amounts harms the earth's climate by warming it up so that the polar ice-caps could melt and result in massive floods. Trees also give out oxygen, which is necessary for life to humans and all animals.

Some rainforest trees grow enormously tall – to over 60 m. Their leaves form the 'canopy', like an umbrella, which blocks out the light so there is fairly little undergrowth on the ground.

The wildlife of Amazonia is amazingly varied and rich. In the late nineteenth century, an English naturalist counted 14,712 species of creature, of which over 8,000 had been unknown. Now well over 100,000 types of animals and birds are known, along with at least 270,000 species of beetle. Probably millions more await discovery.

The native peoples of Amazonia lived there for centuries, but when Europeans arrived about 500 years ago, many were taken into slavery, killed by disease or forced to give up their traditional ways of life. The rainforest is now in serious danger because it is being cut down at a frightening rate to clear land for crops or cattle ranching, to supply the US meat market.

▶ In the Amazon rainforest, an area about the size of eight to ten houses and gardens contains about sixty different species of tree. This is fifteen times as many as would be found in the same area in the forests of Europe or North America.

Giant Sequoias

Two huge types of evergreen conifers, both often called sequoia, are found in the USA. One, the redwood (*Sequoia sempervirens*), is the tallest tree in the world. It grows along a small section of the central coast of California and in central Oregon. The tallest single tree, which grows in the Redwood National Park, in the north-western corner of California, is 112 m high – as tall as St Paul's Cathedral in London.

The sequoia (*Sequoiadendron giganteum*) is the bulkiest of all tree species. The General Sherman tree, in the Sequoia National Park in the Sierra Nevada Mountains, is at least 3,200 years old and could be 4,000. It is not only the biggest sequoia, but is also the most massive living thing on Earth: 83 m tall and a girth (round the trunk) of 24 m.

▶ A sequoia rises like a giant into the sky.

▼ The Tunnel Log, a huge fallen tree, bridges a road in Sequoia National Park.

At Klamath is the Cathedral Tree, where nine trees have grown from one root system, to form a circle like a cathedral. Californians sometimes choose to get married here. Redwoods will regrow from stumps. When a woodsman built himself a cabin of redwood timber, the logs went on sprouting and he had to clip his house regularly, as if it were a hedge.

Singing Dunes

The scientist Ralph Bagnold described how, in the desert, he suddenly and for several minutes heard 'a low-pitched sound' that was so ear-piercing that it drowned out normal speech; this happened particularly on still evenings after a windy day.

What he was hearing was not some strange ceremony nor the working of an unusual machine, but sand dunes 'singing'. Sands in the southern Sahara, the Taklimakan Desert of central Asia and the Rub 'al Khali (Empty Quarter) of Saudi Arabia are known to make these amazing, even frightening, sounds.

Sand is made of grains of the mineral quartz. When grains of sand of the same size are disturbed by the wind or an animal passing by, they begin to move downhill in thin waves, like oil over glass. Sometimes, as the sand moves, a deep, vibrating moan can be heard, which grows to a roar, then dies out as the waves of sand come to rest.

It seems that temperature plays a part in whether or not a dune will 'sing' – the hotter the surface of the sand, the louder the noise it may produce.

Local people have legends to explain the singing dunes. For example, in the southern Sahara, people say that the sound is the laughter of Rul, the djinn (a spirit that has remarkable powers) of the dunes, who will sing to tease travellers who have become confused with fear and thirst.

▼ The movement of a few grains of sand can start a kind of avalanche, which causes a loud noise called 'singing', as the grains of sand grind against each other.

The Namib Desert

The Namib Desert is one of the oldest and driest deserts in the world. It runs for 2,100 km along the Atlantic coast of south-west Africa, from the border between Angola and Namibia to the Orange River. At its widest point it measures 160 km, and at its narrowest it is only 10 km across.

The desert is divided in two by the Kuiseb River. To the south is an immense sea of sand, with crescent, straight and star shaped dunes, some as much as 200 m high. Layers of gravel over a million years old lie under the dunes, and hold the largest single deposit of diamonds in the world.

North of the river are rocky gravel plains. Along the shore, known as the Skeleton Coast, the waters are stormy and dangerous. Many seafarers have lost their ships or even their lives there.

▼ The graceful, S-shaped ridge of a dune at Sossusvlei in the Namib Desert.

Less than 25 mm of rainwater falls along the coastline each year, usually in sudden, heavy storms, and there is often no rain at all. Moisture comes, however, from the dew that forms at night, and from the mists and fogs that roll in over the coast at night every ten days or so. These sometimes reach as far as 50 km inland. The plants and animals found here have adapted to survive in this harsh, dry place and, in some cases, have learned to drink from the mists.

On the gravel plains north of the Kuiseb River is an extraordinary plant that grows nowhere else on earth. This is the *Welwitschia mirabilis*, which can survive for 2,000 years. It takes in moisture through its two leathery, strap-like leaves, which may grow up to 3 m long.

Western Erg of the Sahara

The Sahara in northern Africa covers over 8.5 million sq. km, and is the largest desert in the world. Most people think of the Sahara as a region of rolling dunes but in fact only about a fifth is made up of sand. The rest is bare gravel plains, rocky plateaux, mountains and salt flats. These sandy areas are called 'erg' in Arabic.

The scorching sun makes the Sahara one of the hottest, driest regions on earth, with temperatures often above 38°C during the daytime, while at night the temperature can fall to below freezing point.

The driest parts of the Sahara usually have less than 25 mm of rain a year, and in some years none at all. Where it does rain, the water evaporates into the air rather than seeping into the ground.

▼ A series of wonderfully shaped crescent dunes in the Western Erg of the Sahara Desert.

The wind blows day in and day out, swirling the sand into ever-changing shapes. Some dunes are shaped like crescents, others look like pyramids or are piled up in straight ridges. The sand can be heaped as high as 120 m. In some areas, there are sandstorms for seventy days in each year. People say they have seen walls of sand 480 km wide being whipped along by winds travelling at 48 kph. Whole caravans have disappeared without trace during sandstorms.

About 5,000 years ago, the Sahara was a rich land with buffalo, elephants and giraffes living on it. The people who lived here were herders – their drawings and carvings can still be seen in caves. Then the climate changed and the rivers dried up. Without moisture, the soil broke down so that almost nothing could grow and the area became desert.

Taklimakan Desert

The Taklimakan is a vast, dry, sandy waste in western China. Here pyramid-shaped sand dunes tower 300 m above the plain, and fierce winds can blow up walls of sand to three times that height. The desert is about the same size as New Zealand. The locals have always known it to be a dangerous region. The name Taklimakan means, 'go in and you won't come out'.

Just to the east lies a great bowl of land called the Turpan Depression, which is 154 m below sea-level. This is one of the hottest and lowest places on earth. It hardly ever rains here, and for weeks the temperature can stay at around 40°C. On the eastern fringes of the Depression is the oasis of Turpan itself. Around the area of Turpan are ruined cities founded about 200 BC. They were on the Silk Route, the trade road that ran for about 6,400 km between the Mediterranean countries and China up to the fifteenth century.

▶ The Maiden Togh mountains at the northern edge of the Taklimakan Desert.

▼ Snow and sand make this a barren landscape.

In 1894 the Swedish explorer Sven Hedin with four other men and eight camels, made an agonizing journey across the Taklimakan Desert, through a sand sea with ridges rising to a height of 45 m. The crossing nearly killed them all. As there was no water, they drank methylated spirits, camels' urine and even sheep's blood.

The Atacama Desert

It is hard to imagine a drought lasting for 400 years, but this is what happened in parts of the Atacama Desert in Chile, supposed to be the driest place on earth. In 1971, these areas received some rain for the first time since the late sixteenth century. In Arica, at the northern end of the desert, it never rains at all. It has become a popular holiday resort, fed by piped water from the Andes.

The desert stretches south for about 960 km from the border with Peru. It is generally quite high above sea-level, on average 610 m, and is made up of a series of salt basins with almost no plant life.

Why is the Atacama so dry? Partly because of cold water currents from the Antarctic that cause a lot of fog and cloud but no rain; and partly because the Andes mountains to the east act as a barrier to moist air from the Amazon basin, which might form rain clouds.

▲ Salar San Martin is one of the salt lakes with almost no plant life to be found at the northern end of the Atacama Desert.

The early inhabitants made pictures on the ground – of animals and people and geometric patterns – using dark-coloured stones set in the sand. The biggest is the Giant of the Atacama, near Iquique, who takes up 120 m on a hillside. Nobody knows why these pictures were made. They can be seen best from a distance or, better still, from the air.

▼ In the Valley of the Moon, there may be no rain at all for many years at a stretch.

Painted Desert

Around 200 million years ago, the Painted Desert of Arizona, in the USA, was a broad, swampy floodplain, with hills and volcanic mountains at the edges, on which grew giant cone-bearing trees (conifers). Floods left behind layers of mud, gravel and volcanic ash, which turned to rocks called sandstone and shale. These soaked up minerals and became stained with a rainbow of colours. They were then covered with a large inland sea.

Later, about 65 million years ago, a violent movement of the Earth produced the Rocky Mountains and, at the same time, lifted the land of the Painted Desert above the water-level. The weather did the rest, leaving us with the flat-topped mesas that we see today. (See also the Petrified Forest, page 31.)

▼ Did some giant with a liking for colour take a brush to create stripes across the mountains of the Painted Desert?

Dinosaurs roamed the area. The largest of these was *Postosuchus*, about 5 m long, with huge, jagged teeth and a bony crest running along its body. The 3-m *Metosopaurus* was an amphibian, which caught fish with its long jaws. It was probably the main prey of the *Phytosaurus*, which had a snout like a crocodile's that was about 1 m long.

The Badlands

This area of knife-edge ridges, deep gullies, narrow, flat-topped hills and desert which seems to stretch endlessly to the horizon, is well named. Both the Sioux people and the Europeans gave it the same name in their own languages. Lying in the south-west of South Dakota and in the north-west of Nebraska, USA, the landscape seems empty and is blisteringly hot.

The plateau that is now the Badlands started to form about 80 million years ago. It was then a shallow sea measuring about 15,500 sq. km. The uplift that created the Rocky Mountains about 65 million years ago also pushed up this area. The water ran off and, as the region slowly became drier, took the topsoil and some of the rocks with it. Erosion is still going on – Vampire Peak is being shortened by about 15 cm a year.

▶ The flat-topped hills and desert seem to go on forever in the Badlands.

▼ The layers of sediment from the earlier sea are clearly visible here.

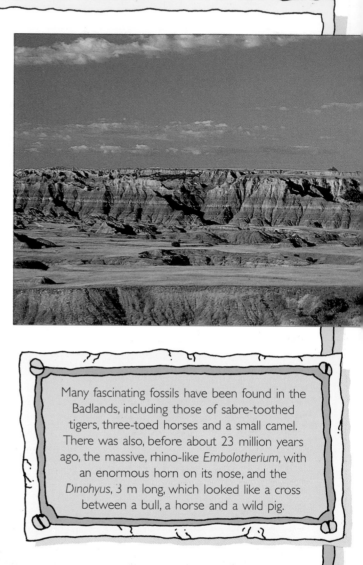

Many fascinating fossils have been found in the Badlands, including those of sabre-toothed tigers, three-toed horses and a small camel. There was also, before about 23 million years ago, the massive, rhino-like *Embolotherium*, with an enormous horn on its nose, and the *Dinohyus*, 3 m long, which looked like a cross between a bull, a horse and a wild pig.

The Dry Valleys, Antarctica

Valleys without snow or ice are not unusual – except in the polar regions. Although ice covers almost all of Antarctica, there are three dry valleys there, on the mainland of the continent to the east of the Ross Ice Shelf and on McMurdo Sound. They are named the Taylor, Wright and Victoria Dry Valleys.

These dry valleys are steep-sided, U-shaped basins carved out by glaciers that have long since melted. Huge, brown or black in colour and free of any plant life, the dry valleys have been described as 'bare stony troughs'.

It takes millions of years for ice to build up to the massive weight that now covers most of the Antarctic, to an average depth of 3,000 m. In the Dry Valleys, though, very little snow falls; the amount is about equal to 25 mm of rain a year. When snow does fall, it is blown away by the dry winds or melted in the surrounding rocks, which take in heat from the sun.

Each of the valleys has some salt lakes. The largest is Lake Vanda, which is more than 60 m deep and has a layer of ice on top that is 4 m thick. The temperature of the water at the bottom is a warm 25°C because the ice on top of the water stops heat from escaping.

▲ View from the summit of Mount Brunhilde, looking over Wright Dry Valley, where some ice formations called frost polygons can be seen. In the far distance is the Olympus range of mountains.

In the cold, dry air of the valleys, animal and plant material is preserved for a long time, just as meat keeps well in a freezer. The Dry Valleys are scattered with the preserved bodies of seals that probably died hundreds or even thousands of years ago.

Rainbow Bridge Word Search

```
N V I C T O R I A J
T A E R G S A R S E Y E
I L E T L E N I A R E Y E T
L K S Y H G N I P E E A A T
E I H A C E A N D R Y A R S B I
Y P A O R E G N I R R A B A O T I Y
S P L A A E P U R E P P O R U C E G
E L E I W M Y           C A R P Y K S
S E H S R A A           A R I C A A O
Y H T A E D K H         C A N A L N N N
```

3 LETTERS
BIG
JET
YAK
SKY
DRY
RAY
DAM
THE
KAN

4 LETTERS
LAKE
EYRE
PERU
SEAS
ALPS
BORA
ROCK
THAI
ASIA
RAIN
PEAK
YETI
GLEN
KHOA
PING
HELL
NOSE

5 LETTERS
ARICA
AUYAN
BAYEI
CANAL
COAST
DEATH
AYERS
SPIKE
GREAT
RANGE

6 LETTERS
VALLEY
SHAPES
ARCHES

7 LETTERS
ROARING
SARAWAK

8 LETTERS
VICTORIA

9 LETTERS
BARRINGER

Answers can be found on page 111

Index

Picture Acknowledgements

t = top b = below
Audience Planners: Satour 59t,
59b; USTTA 24b, cover & 49b,
71t, 71b; Wyoming Travel
Commission cover & 24t.
**Australian Tourist
Commission:** cover & 37t, 37b,
38a, 38b, 93t, cover & 93b, 94t,
94b, 95t, 95b, 97b; Andreas
Huelsmann 96; Nick Rains 97t.
Bodø Arrangement A/S: 33t.
J. Allan Cash: 22t. **China
National Tourist Office:** cover
& 78b, 78t, 88b. **Consorzio
Frasassi:** cover & 73t, 73b.
Corbis-Bettman: S. Hunter
49t; Massimo Orione 50b, 91t.
Christina Dodwell: 83t, 83b.
Hulton Deutsch Collection:
39. **Icelandair:** cover & 23t,
56b. **Image Bank:** 17b, 31b;
Walter Bibikow 25t; Joseph B.

Brignolo 52b; Gerard
Champlong 54b; T. Chinami
65; Giuliano Colliva cover &
70t, 100b; Per Eide 77t, 77b;
FotoWorld 81t; Larry Dale
Gordon 47t; David Jeffrey 81b;
Steve Krongard 88t; Don
Landwehrle 106b; Stephen
Marks 70b, 100t; Kaz Mori 6 &
99t; Nick Nicholson 31t; Martí
Pié cover & 62; Andrea
Pistolesi cover & 19t, 19b, 79t,
99b; Chuck Place 92b; Jake Rajs
cover & 90, 106t; Anne Rippy
cover, 1 & 36t; Guido Albert
Rossi 10t, 14b, 36b, 40t, 40b,
cover & 50t, 54t; Bernard
Russell 17t; Steve Satushek 91b;
Juan Silva 69b; Stock-photos
82; Weinberg-Clark 92t. **Roger
Kohn:** 48t. **Jiri Lochman:** 43t,
43b. **Mansell Collection:** cover
& 11t, 14t. **Mary Evans Picture
Library:** 33b. **Mountain
Camera:** John Cleare 61t, 61b;
Colin Monteath 6 & 58t, 58b,
107. **New Zealand Tourist

Board:** 25b, 75t, 75b, 79b.
Kathleen O'Donnell: 16b.
Österreich Werbung: 72t,
7&72b.
Oxford Scientific Films: C.C.
Lockwood, **Earth Scenes** 55b;
David B. Fleetham 34t; Nick
Gordon, **Survival Anglia** 98;
Peter Parks 34b; Will & Deni
McIntyre 44t. **Robert Harding
Picture Library:** 9, 10b, 11b,
15t, cover, 7 & 15b, 16t, 20b,
30t, 30b, 41, 51t, 55t, 60b, 64t,
64b, 66, 85t, 85b, 86t, 86B, 102,
103t, 103b, 105b; J.R. Ashford
68t; Julia Bayne 84t; Martin
Burton 51b; S.H.& H.D.
Cavanaugh 84b; G. & P.
Corrigan 89b; Explorer 13t;
Robert Francis cover & 26b,
27b, 67, 76; Paul Freestone
cover & 101; Jon Gardey 60t;
Tony Gervis 105t; Kim Hart
23b, cover & 56t; David
Hughes 13b; F. Jack Jackson
26t; Robert McLeod 6 & 104;
Louise Murray 74t;

Christopher Rennie 80b;
Sassoon 48b, 57t; E. Simanor
27t; David Tokeley 89t; Tony
Waltham 16t, 74b, Nedra
Westwater 52t; Dave Willis 57t.
**Russia & Republics Photo
Library:** Mark Wadlow 42b.
Science Photo Library: David
Hardy 22b; Francis Leroy,
Biocosmos 35b; NASA 32;
Novosti Press Agency 42t;
David Parker 20t; Peter Ryan
35t. **Sólarfilma:** 12t, cover &
12b. **South American Pictures:**
Peter Francis 104t; David
Horwell 68b; Kimball Morrison
69t; Tony Morrison 16b, 2, 28b,
47b, 80t; Chris Sharp 46.
**South Australian Tourist
Commission:** 29t, 29b. **SPL:**
Ned Haines 8. **Swiss National
Tourist Office:** SVZ/L.
Degonda cover & 63.
**Turkish National Tourist
Office:** cover & 21t, 21b.
Zooid Pictures: cover & 44b,
45, 53t, 53b, 87t, 87b